FINISHED IT

Keep your forks!

The **BEST** is always

yet to come!

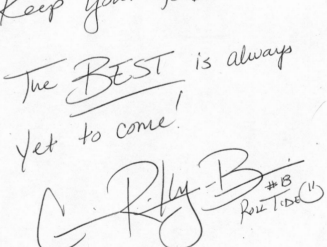

C. Riley B #B
Roll Tide

FINISHED IT

A TEAM'S JOURNEY TO WINNING IT ALL

CASSIE REILLY-BOCCIA

FINISHED IT
A TEAM'S JOURNEY TO WINNING IT ALL

iUniverse books may be ordered through booksellers or by contacting:

iUniverse
1663 Liberty Drive
Bloomington, IN 47403
www.iuniverse.com
1-800-Authors (1-800-288-4677)

.

ISBN: 978-1-4917-4843-5 (sc)
ISBN: 978-1-4917-4844-2 (hc)
ISBN: 978-1-4917-4842-8 (e)

Library of Congress Control Number: 2014917293

Printed in the United States of America.

iUniverse rev. date: 11/14/2014

"Nothing of me is original, I am the combined
effort of everyone I've ever known."
– Chuck Palahniuk –

For my parents, Chris and Donna
Thank you, thank you, thank you. We sometimes take for
granted the love and support our parents give because it is
unwavering and appears never ending. I am overwhelmed when
I think about what my life would be like without your love.
How different my journey would have been had it been absent
of your support. I will never forget sitting in the hotel room at
age 13, watching the WCWS on ESPN, looking to the two
of you and saying, "I want to do that one day." That 'day'
would have never come without you both. Love you guys.

To every coach I've ever had to honor to play for,
Thank you for guiding me through this amazing sport and
helping me fall more and more in love with the game.

To every teammate I've ever had the privilege of
sharing a jersey with and playing along side,
Thank you for the inspiration and motivation for this book. I am
the person I am today because of each and every one of you.

To my family and friends,
You have made this journey complete. Without all of you
to share in the victories and defeats something vital would
have been missing from this entire experience. Thank you for
always understanding how special this game was to me.

CONTENTS

FOREWORD

There is something so pure and beautiful about the game of softball. For anyone who has played the game you can almost immediately smell the freshly cut grass, feel the dirt under your cleats, and see yourself standing between those crisp white lines. You know the joy of a win and the sting of loss. Softball is more than a game; it is a passion and a way of life.

Softball has been a cornerstone of my life for as long as I can remember. Playing a sport that is riddled with failure gives athletes like myself many tools to succeed later in life. As much as I learned on the field about overcoming failure, working hard, and mental toughness, it will never measure up to the life lessons that I learned off the field. In fact it will never come close to what I've learned from the people that shaped me, challenged me, and changed me during my four years at the University of Alabama. What I realized during my collegiate career is the beauty of softball goes so far beyond hitting a ball with a bat. Softball is about learning and growing, sharing in achievements, and building relationships. It's about creating a bond with a special group of women that will last a lifetime.

Finished It, gives you a glimpse into the life and experiences of a collegiate softball player, specifically the trials and triumphs of the 2012 Alabama Softball National Championship team. This book will take you on a journey of the final day of the

Crimson Tide's season in Oklahoma City from the eyes of first baseman, Cassie Reilly-Boccia. Each chapter will provide you, the reader, with flashbacks of a life lesson that guided the team to the SEC's first national championship in softball. *Finished It,* brings selfless themes into the forefront of athletics.

If you are looking for a book that will teach you the fundamentals of softball, this isn't it. If you are looking for a book that will give you inspiration to do better and think more about others than yourself, this is the one for you. I believe that every softball player, young athlete or coach should read this book because it will help develop an athlete as a whole person, not just a player. It will also help you realize that winning does not just happen, and it's not just an accumulation of all the hard work you put into your sport. Winning is the result of life experiences throughout your entire athletic career that give you the desire to push a little bit harder and finish a little bit stronger.

We are taught as softball players to leave the sport a little bit better than when we found it. *Finished It* encourages us to do the same, and at the same time is leaving you a little better than when you found it.

-Kayla Braud
ESPN Analyst, National Champion,
Senior CLASS Award Winner, 3-Time
All-American, 4-Time All-SEC

PROLOGUE

June 7, 2012 12:28 am

I rubbed the skin of the bright yellow softball with my left hand. It had just come in contact with the damp grass after being hit in foul territory down the first base line. It hadn't rained since the fourth inning and by now the field seemed back to normal for the most part. The excitement from the stands faintly echoed in my ear. I looked up at my pitcher, Jackie Traina, and said calmly, "Nice job Jack, let's get this one right here."

'Let's get this one.' As if this 'one' was just another batter in the season. I've told her that hundreds of times in our two years playing together. 'Let's get this one.' I jogged back to my defensive spot at first base. Strategically positioned for this particular batter, for this one.

I glanced at the scoreboard before I turned around to get into my ready stance. It was the top of the seventh inning in the third and final game of the 2012 NCAA Women's Softball National Championship Series. A best of three series between the softball programs from the University of Alabama and the University of Oklahoma. Each team had claimed one victory apiece in the previous two days.

Two outs. Two strikes. As home team, the Alabama Crimson Tide was leading 5-4 and playing defense with the national player of the year at the plate for Oklahoma. As I watched the hitter step into the batter's box and I looked around the field at my teammates, it was hard to believe that this would be the last game for me and the five other seniors. The last time we would wear the script Alabama "A" on our jerseys.

Playing in a situation like this is like walking a tightrope in your mind. In order to stay balanced on the rope, you have to stay in the present. It requires the utmost sense of focus and control, all the while willing yourself to remain calm. I kept thinking to myself, 'Stay in the present, stay in the present.' Losing focus for a split second leaves you vulnerable and at the mercy of uncertainty. You become in danger of permitting a poisonous thought to creep into your mind; 'We are only one strike away from winning a national championship.' It approaches you like a whisper, almost too faint to recognize. The moment you acknowledge the venom's presence, its paralyzing effects have already begun to take their toll. As you fall from the tightrope, a rush of butterflies will soar from your stomach to the rest of your body; your arms become numb, your hands tremor, and your legs go weak. Your heart rate skyrockets, pounding at a distracting rhythm inside your constricted chest. The thoughts in your head become deafening. The calls from your teammate just ten feet away will sound like a distant murmur. Your breathing becomes irregular, your eyes widen, nervously darting from one place to the next. It is alarming to realize how much your body is at the mercy of your mind in this situation. Deep breath. 'Stay in the present, this pitch is coming to you.' I'd say to myself. Deep breath.

It requires an enormous amount of mental strength to battle your mind and regain balance on the tightrope. Being in control of both your mind and your body is one tool every athlete who has played at a high level can relate to. Just like every physical aspect of the game, this skill comes from great coaching, practice, and experience.

I looked over at our second baseman and said, "Hey Danae! This one is coming to us on the right side, right here; nothing gets by us."

We made eye contact and she gave me a reassuring nod. It was too slight for anyone in the stands to notice. It is amazing how teammates can have such complex conversations on the field without saying a single word.

Deep breath. 'Stay in the present.' The slightest reminder was enough to keep me on my tightrope.

I took a step toward our pitcher, "Here we go, Jack! There is nobody better than you, you're gonna win this pitch, we're with you! I believe it right here, right now, Jack. Win this <u>one</u>.*"*

Deep breath. 'Stay in the present.' Walk the tightrope... steady... balance... calm... focused... in control.

I heard the Alabama fans across the field above the third base dugout. I heard the Oklahoma fans to my left above the first base dugout. I heard the strained voices of my teammates, coaches, managers, and trainers screaming encouragements at Jackie from across the infield. I heard the OU dugout doing the same for their batter. I could feel my heart pounding but my breathing was steady. With conviction in their voices I heard the continual reassurance between our infield and pitcher. Our catcher, Kendall Dawson, remained calm and relaxed. She was the leader whom everyone on the field could look towards as a calming presence. Her voice remained solid and confident, completely absent of a quiver. I faintly heard the outfielders chatter, speaking to each other and to Jackie. I heard the scratch of my metal cleats as they scraped against the dirt on the field below me.

Deep breath.

I no longer heard the fans.

Deep breath.

No more cheers from the dugout.

Jackie got the sign and she started her motion.

Deep breath.

The field went still.

I planted my left foot, followed by my right. I was in my ready stance; a position that had became so familiar to me. I barely noticed the crunch of the dirt under my cleats anymore.

One more deep breath as I crouched low. Glove out in front, heels off the ground, ready to move. 'Nothing by you, this pitch is coming to you, this pitch, this pitch, this pitch.' My heartbeat was somewhere off in the distance. My vision narrowed, nothing else existed except this pitch, except this <u>one</u>.

INTRODUCTION

"AT FIRST THEY'LL ASK YOU WHY YOU'RE DOING IT, THEN THEY'LL ASK YOU HOW YOU DID IT."

As a member of the Alabama Crimson Tide softball team, I always got asked the question, "Why do you want it so badly?" It was asked by people who didn't fully understand. People who couldn't wrap their minds around this crazy dream of ours. "It won't change your life, *it's just a game*." they would say. Maybe there is some sense in that. Softball is technically a 'game.' And winning a national championship wouldn't significantly change our lives. We wouldn't wake up the morning after winning and suddenly find ourselves rich and famous. It wouldn't magically wipe away all the struggles and heartaches from the rest of our lives. However, there was one thing I was sure they were wrong about, this wasn't *just a game*, to us, this was so much more.

Maybe it was a desire for a legacy. Every human is ingrained with a yearning to leave something of themselves behind. However, those who find their passion interpret this insatiable desire not as just such, but also as a responsibility, an obligation, and a need.

I always had this idea that the first team to win a national championship in softball from Alabama would be cemented in history. I thought that somehow if we won it, we'd never have to experience the inevitable sting felt by athletes going through withdrawal from their sport and team their first few years after graduation. As if the trophy would keep us immune from these feelings. Winning Alabama's first Women's College World Series (WCWS) would be ours and ours alone. It would not be a statistical record that someone else could break. It was something that no one could ever take away from us, our little mark on history.

In June 2011, at the end of my junior year, our season had just ended with two embarrassing losses to our SEC rival in the semi-final series of the WCWS. It was then that I finally realized the answer to the question 'why.' I wanted to win a national championship because I wanted *us* to know what it felt like. That's it. Seems simple enough, I'm sure a lot of people would like to know what it feels like. Unlike others though, we were in a position to make it happen. We had all the ingredients at our disposal to make our dream a reality. I wanted us to know so badly what the celebration felt like. We had watched so many teams before celebrate the infamous last out. On *that* field. Under *those* lights at the iconic Hall of Fame Stadium in Oklahoma City.

For a team to know they had won it all and to know that everything they had sacrificed, the hours, the sweat, the aches and pains, the trials and tribulations, had amounted to this would be an incredible feeling. Imagining that it would be the best possible feeling any of them could have ever experienced. The reason this feeling would be so special would be because the desire to experience it resonated not just with myself but with my teammates as well. I knew this was something that was unattainable without my teammates. It is not possible in softball to win a national championship on your own, not as a pitcher, hitter, position player, or coach. Which is why I craved the feeling even more. I wanted *us* to know what it felt like to be the last team celebrating in the entire country. I wanted *us* to dog pile, to take the iconic picture in front of the scoreboard, to feel like the nine-year-old girls that fell head over heels in love with this game. I wanted this team to be a part of something bigger than ourselves as individuals and experience something we never could have achieved on our own.

I feel like I have an insurmountable debt to this game. However, it is not a burden nor does a feeling of guilt accompany it. Instead, I feel like this game has helped me become the best version of myself. This game has introduced me to some of the best people, has given me some of the best moments, and has provided me with endless opportunities to be successful for the rest of my life. Therefore, any time I am able to share stories of our journey or any time I see a young girl say she has been inspired by the way we played, I feel like I am making a payment to this debt. And it feels incredibly satisfying to pay it back.

Because of this, I feel compelled to tell this story. Perhaps those who share the same love for the game can get something from this book. I am not an expert on coaching, the mental game, nor softball. However, what I do know is this story I'm about to tell, it worked. And although there is no perfect blueprint for 'How to Win a National Championship,' I do feel there is a right way to play this game. Sports are played at their best when they are played with passion, heart, and a genuine love for the game and for one another. That's how *we* played this game. We knew in order to win it all, it would take leadership, selflessness, traditions, celebrations, adversity, and a supreme confidence in everything we did. It would require a willingness to fail, a willingness to give it all, and an extraordinarily ability to finish. If there was something to be learned in all of this, I wanted to share it. This is our story.

I woke up the morning of June 6, 2012 and the first thought that came to mind was, "The next time we go to sleep, we could be national champions." We now had it dangling right before our faces; the opportunity that has eluded so many who have come before us. It was the chance to reach the pinnacle of our sport, to celebrate on that field, under those lights after we had exhausted ourselves on the field in battle. My mind drifted to the potential post-game celebration but I quickly had to snap myself out of it, 'Stay in the present.' That phrase would inevitably repeat itself in my head many more times throughout the day.

I'd like to say I got a good night sleep the night before because at the time I thought I did, but in reality, I had the championship game on my mind the entire time. My roommate for the week was Ryan Iamurri. The 4'10" second baseman hailed from Naples, Florida. Ryan was a winner through and through and always seemed to know exactly what the team needed to succeed. I was very grateful to have her as my roommate for the entire World Series.

Being one of the final two teams left at the WCWS was uncharted territory for Alabama Softball. In its sixteen-year history and seven previous trips to this championship event, the Crimson Tide softball program had never made it past the semi-final round. During that week as roommates, Ryan and I took time to debrief and dissect the emotional ups and downs that came with competing at the WCWS. We began to recognize a certain pattern of anxiety that arose. It did not stem from a fear of failure or a doubt of success, but more of a yearning to know. I can only compare this feeling to watching an exciting movie, sitting on the edge of your seat, intently caught in suspense, hungry for the satisfaction of the outcome. We wanted to know how our story was going to end. We wanted to know so badly who would be the last team celebrating in Oklahoma City.

Throughout the week, Ryan and I made it a habit of scribbling notes with our finger into the fog of the bathroom mirror after showering. The phrases and notes would only come to life once the fog returned the following night, they remained invisible to us during the day. As I stepped out of the shower the night before our final game, the mirror was covered with sayings in both mine and Ryan's handwriting. Sayings that we were too afraid to say out loud, words that clearly broke the code of, 'staying in the present.' "Imagine what the celebration will be like!", "Three more wins and we will win it all", were just a few that decorated the fog covered mirror. As I surveyed the mirror on the night of June 5th I noticed a small space at the bottom that remained blank. I took my finger and wrote the last and final note of our stay in Oklahoma City: "By this time tomorrow night, we'll KNOW!"

"We'll KNOW!" We will finally finish the chapter on this amazing ride. No matter the outcome, tonight, June 6th, will mark the final game played in the 2012 NCAA softball season. One game, under the lights. I had this feeling like nothing could stand in our way, we had momentum on our side from a win the night before and that gave me so much confidence in my team for tonight's game. I knew we could do this, there was not a doubt in my mind that anything would stand in our way.

As I got out of bed I checked the weather app on my phone. It was going to be a fairly cool and overcast day for Oklahoma City. I finally got to the hour-by-hour report for 7:00pm, the time our game was supposed to start. The forecast called for rain.

CHAPTER 1

"IT ALL STARTS AT THE TOP."

It was good to be with my dog and back home seeing my family. Just four days earlier we woke up one win away from making it to the championship finals at the 2011 Women's College World Series in Oklahoma City. That night we went to bed with two losses, an embarrassing 16-2 run rule in the first game of the day and a 9-2 beating for the nightcap. Both losses were to our SEC rival, the Florida Gators. Absolutely nothing about those games left a good taste in our mouths. I hated losing more than anything, we all did.

I can remember exactly where I was and what I was doing when I got the phone call. It was June 9, 2011 and I was in my dad's old pickup truck driving home from my aunt's house. My dog, Jake, an 80-pound Sheppard and Black Labrador mix was enjoying life, riding shotgun with his head out the window on a record high temperature day in New York.

My phone rang with an incoming call from a 205 area code indicating the call was coming from Tuscaloosa, Alabama. I answered the phone (using my hands free device as to not break New York State driving laws). As I said hello,

I manually cranked the windows up so I could hear the incoming caller.

"Hello?"

"Hey, Cass. It's Murphy."

"Hey, Murph! How are you doing?"

"Cass, I've got some news and it's not good."

Then all I heard was sobbing. Our head coach, Patrick Murphy, our leader, the guy who always knew what to do and knew what to say could not hold back his tears. I immediately thought of my teammates and their families. Since our loss four days ago the Alabama softball family was driving and flying long distances traveling back home to Oregon, Florida, Georgia, Missouri, and Texas. My first thought was worst-case scenario; did something happen to one of them in their travels? My stomach sank and my heart pounded uncontrollably in anticipation of this 'bad news.' What was probably only a few seconds of waiting felt so much longer.

"I got offered the job at LSU and I took it."

He could barely get the sentence out. And I hate to say it, but I actually felt relief. Everyone was safe and okay. My brain quickly tried to wrap itself around this new reality. Our coach was leaving Alabama to coach at Louisiana State University. I had no idea what to say. He was still noticeably upset on the other end of the line.

"Murph, are you okay?"

"No." was his only response.

Still, I had no idea what to say. My brain was searching for the 'right' response but everything I was coming up with would have been wildly inappropriate at the time. "*If you're not okay, then don't go! What are you thinking?! What are you doing?! Please don't leave! You belong at Bama!*" Clearly nothing in my arsenal of thoughts was rational at the time. Any rhyme or reason my mind had to offer was fogged by absolute shock.

The rest of the conversation was fairly short. I found out that our beloved associate head coach, Alyson "Aly" Habetz, would be going with him as well. Her entire family whom we all adored resided in Louisiana, just a short drive from the LSU campus in Baton Rouge. She'd be going home, and that was understandable. I told Murph that I knew he had to do what was best for him and that we would miss the both of them like crazy. I hung up the phone and tried to quickly fast forward in my head to the next time I'd see my coaches; well I guess they weren't 'mine' anymore. LSU would travel to Tuscaloosa that upcoming spring season and play as the visiting team versus Alabama. Our coaches, well their coaches, would be there, wearing purple and gold. In the other dugout. Cheering for another team, for other girls. Murphy would be in his third base coaches' box right next to us in our third base dugout. Would we talk with them? Laugh with them? It made me cringe.

There is a certain type of venom reserved in an Alabama fan's heart for those who wear purple and gold. It is on full display during football games and clearly trickles down to every sporting event between the two schools. "Are our fans going to boo them?" The thought raced through my mind. The coaches that had started the Alabama Softball program and brought it from it's infancy to a full-blown national title contending powerhouse were going to be enemies in the house they built.

It made my heart hurt to think about. I quickly pushed those thoughts out of my head. I wanted nothing more than to be with my team. I wanted us all together to deal with this and figure out a plan on how to handle it. Instead, we were all home, spread thin across the country.

It is important to understand why this was such a big deal to us. Every year at some point, Aly would talk about how 'It all starts at the top.' She would point out how everything Murphy did, the way he acted, his work ethic, his passion for softball, it would resonate throughout the entire Alabama Softball program. He cared deeply about each and every one of his players. He took pride in being an influential figure in our lives. He was the one responsible for providing all of the players with the unbelievable opportunity to play softball at Alabama. My teammate, Jazlyn Lunceford once said that Murphy had one of the coolest jobs in the country because he, "Got to make girls' dreams come true."

Murphy had a brain that could remember everything. He especially never forgot a name. He made everyone feel so special. I started to realize that my teammates and I were also trying to make the effort to remember names, faces, and details of others' lives.

"How did your daughter do in her championship game last weekend?"

"How's that wrist feeling? Finally able to play again?"

These would be some of the questions I'd notice our team asking anyone from reporters to five-year-old fans that came to the ballpark. You can be genuinely concerned about someone and their life but when you make the effort to show it, when you go above and beyond, people take notice. It makes them feel good inside and people felt good when they were surrounded by our team, especially when they met Murphy or Aly. I'm not sure our team would have known exactly how to do these things unless we saw our leaders do it first.

Aly would tell us all the time that we should show respect to everyone we met and came in contact with not because of who *they* were but because of who *we* were. Both Aly and Murphy exuded class and dignity in everything they did. They were model human beings to look up to and aspire to be like. I couldn't think of two people better fit to mold young student athletes on a daily basis.

The power these two had of influencing others did not stem from fear. I've seen this happen when certain leaders walk into a room. Everyone makes an effort to cater to them and please them because they are nervous of the consequences if they don't. Murphy was able to lead in such a way that everyone embraced his vision. He lived what he preached. He was the one getting to know everyone we came in contact with from the University president and ESPN reporters, to airport personnel and workers cleaning up the stadium after a game. He believed in appreciation and was thankful for the things people did for him. I can guarantee you every person who has played for him has a thank you card from him for something. He made sure you knew he appreciated you in some way, shape, or form.

There is a tremendous amount of pressure that accompanies this power. Murphy and Aly's ripple effect touched more lives than they can even fathom. Needless to say, Coach Murphy and Coach Aly made our program what is was, they made us a family. They built the program around a core of strong morals that included having an attitude of gratitude in everything we did, showing class, displaying character, and respecting an opponent at all costs. Murphy was there from the very first game in this program's history and I guess everyone felt like he should be there until the end of his career too.

It was an unfair assumption in some ways. How can you expect someone to sacrifice their life if it wasn't exactly what they wanted? Even after Murphy's phone call, I felt weird being angry. How could I be angry? This was *their* job, *their* earnings, *their* life. When Coach Murphy and Coach Aly left for Louisiana State University, there was a sadness that swept through the entire Alabama Softball family. Fans who had been there from the start who were so closely connected to this program must have felt that their only son and daughter left the nest. People took Murphy and Aly in as one of their own. An alumna's Facebook status that night read, "Alabama Softball will never, ever be the same!" I couldn't agree more and that worried me.

Anyone who has ever played for a team knows how similar a team is to a family. Murphy used to tell us all the time that regardless of whether we got the big hit with the bases loaded or struck out, he would always love us. I think the feeling was mutual with him. Regardless of where our coaches' next journey would take them, our team was still going to love them. We were all going to miss calling them, "ours."

It can be quite comical to picture the scenario I found myself in after Murphy's phone call. I was driving in that rickety old pick-up truck with no air-conditioning on one of the hottest days in the history of New York State and my oversized dog was right smack in the middle of his shedding season. I was on the verge of tears, sweating, with dog hair getting caught in my mouth on every deep breath I tried to take to calm myself down.

The last thing Murphy told me before he got off the phone was that I was the first person from the team he had contacted. He was going to call one of the other seniors next and I'd probably be hearing from them soon. So I sat in silence and waited. I didn't cry. I just had this awful feeling in my stomach as I drove. I had to tell my parents. As soon as my mom said

"Hello" on the other line, I too started crying and probably sounded very similar to my mom as Murphy sounded to me only moments earlier.

"Cassie, are you okay?!" My poor mother thought I was in an accident and all I could tell her was that I was 'Okay.' I finally blurted out that Murph and Aly were leaving Alabama and becoming the new coaches at LSU. I think mom experienced the same feeling I did when I first heard the news; relieved that everyone was alright and not in danger, but still in disbelief.

The rest of the ride home I sat impatiently waiting a call from one of my teammates. Whether you're a dog person or not, one thing is very clear: they can have a special connection to a human's emotion. My dog, Jake knew right away something was not right. He laid down in the front seat of the truck cab and put his head on my lap. There are not many things that can make you feel better during a time like that, but having my dog by my side was exactly what I needed.

The chaos of that night passed by in a blur. I knew the rising seniors needed to get on the same page. I realized on my drive home that this would be the first thing we had to deal with as a senior class. Just days earlier we were juniors standing in Hall of Fame Stadium in Oklahoma City fighting for a chance to get to the national championship series. Now we were lost and struggling to find our way out of a tangled mess.

We made sure a senior spoke to every person on our team. We had a clear and concise message. We were going to be smart about what we posted to social media, we weren't going to make hasty, rushed decisions about our future on the team until the dust settled, and above all else we were going to stick together and we were going to get through this. Then junior, Kayla Braud called me and said that the two of us should conference call each incoming freshman. I told her it was a great idea and agreed to be her accomplice with these inevitable, highly emotional phone conversations.

When you are getting recruited to a program, you get to know the coach and their staff first. You then meet the team on a few visits here and there afterwards. It is the coaching staff that you build the relationship with prior to your arrival. When Kayla and I spoke to these incoming freshmen they were devastated. That year we had two girls coming from over ten hours away, they had taken a leap of faith to leave their family and now it seemed like they were falling without a parachute. We assured them all that the team was there with a safety net. We made sure every freshman knew that everything we preached to them about Alabama Softball was real. It was imperative that they knew we cared about each other above anything else, we were resilient and we would face this adversity by staying united.

I used three different phones and a computer that day to get in touch with teammates past, present, and future, as well as compliance and administrative members at Alabama, former coaches of mine, family, and friends. The outpouring of support was unbelievable. Everyone in our lives knew how important these two people were to us and it was like a little piece of everyone's heart got tugged on that day. If you ever had the pleasure to meet Coach Murphy or Coach Aly, you would understand, there is just something special about them.

Everyone experienced mixed emotions that day. Some people were sad, angry, hurt, confused and bewildered. No matter who you were, the common denominator among anyone who knew anything about softball was utter shock. I don't believe even LSU softball fans saw this coming. 'Patrick

Murphy' was trending worldwide on twitter that night, the LSU Tigers sports homepage had a picture of their two new coaches wearing photo-shopped purple shirts. It was a hard pill to swallow.

The following three days were a whirlwind. Rumors and confusion flew as to why the coaches left in the first place. Why LSU? Who were the new coaches going to be? Were current players on the team going to transfer? Like I said, absolute chaos. Still, throughout this difficult time I commended my teammates. There was not a single thing said on Facebook or Twitter that was inappropriate or out of line. Despite being up to a thousand miles a part, our team was able to stay in touch and provide the support and comfort we needed.

We endured watching Patrick Murphy's press conference welcoming him to LSU. "He looks nervous," was the first text I got from a teammate when the press conference began. I smirked but quickly felt incredibly sad. We all knew Murph so well. I still couldn't wrap my mind around him coaching other student-athletes. That wasn't a fair thought, but still, it was there. We couldn't help but be happy for Aly. Her entire family was at the press conference cheering and whistling when she walked in. The second text I got from a teammate read, "She finally gets to be with her family, he brought her home."

On June 12, 2011, three days after that initial phone call and two days after the press conference, my phone that was sitting quietly on the kitchen table lit up with yet another call. The phone read 'Patrick Murphy' as it made a loud buzzing noise. I blankly starred at the phone. I scanned my brain as to why he would be calling. I came up with nothing. I didn't know why he was trying to contact me, he was someone else's coach, he was no longer my coach.

"Hello?"

"Hey, Cass. It's Murphy."

"Hey, Murph. What's up?"

"I got some more news for you…"

I couldn't tell if he was laughing or crying but there was an anxious tremor to his voice.

"What's that Mur—"

"We're coming back."

His words echoed with such intensity through the phone. Life hit me with another surprise that I did not see coming, knocking me clear off my tightrope. This was an outcome that I did not think was possible.

Everything Murphy and Aly had instilled in us throughout the years leading up to these three days came to fruition in each and everyone of us. We had stuck together through this difficult time and moved forward into the 2012 season knowing that we could handle anything that was thrown our way.

Almost one year to the date later, I was getting in my ready stance. I was steadying myself for *one* more batter, *one* more out, *one* last pitch.

I left my hotel room on the fourth floor and heard a buzzing coming from the main lobby below. Stepping into the glass elevator, I could finally see the source of noise. The main atrium of the hotel was energetically filled with over a hundred of our family and friends. There were so many familiar faces that came to support us on our journey in Oklahoma City. On the final day of the season, they all joined in a pep-rally to see us off to lunch.

It is an incredible feeling to have so many people share your dream with you. I found myself overwhelmed at times with the outpouring of support and encouragement I received. When playing a team sport there is a certain special camaraderie that develops. It is something that has been difficult for me to effectively describe in words. That same closeness occurs with the families of your teammates. It is a special bond held strongly together through the sport of softball. It is a connection that will be there long after our days on the field are over. Being successful in a sport is very fulfilling, however it wouldn't mean nearly as much if we didn't have our loved ones there to celebrate and share the excitement with us.

As I rode down the elevator and surveyed the crowded lobby through the glass walls, I couldn't help but be thankful. I couldn't help but feel I owed so much to all those people in that lobby. I couldn't attempt to calculate the number of miles traveled to tournaments, practices, and lessons, nor the money spent, and the time and effort put into all of us. Their investment in our dream was concrete and never wavered. Solidified by the many family birthday parties missed and the countless vacation days taken, the wear and tear from their sacrifices never showed. Instead, all we ever saw was their unconditional love and never-ending support. Playing a sport at a high level takes a lot of sacrifice on the part of the athlete, yet not everyone sees or notices the sacrifice on the part of all the family members. Our success was just as much their success.

I always felt excitement on the day of a game. It was a very distinct feeling, one that could be confused with nervousness. Both excitement and nervousness cause the infamous butterflies to arise in the stomach. However, the two feelings could not be any further apart from one another. I firmly believe that any nervousness that is experienced stems from a fear of failure. My excitement on the other hand came from possessing the courage to fail.

Although these two feelings seem one in the same, they are not. I've had coaches in the past tell me, 'Don't be afraid to fail.' Failure is like a rabid animal locked away in a cage. I picture this oversized dog with muscles protruding through his fur, baring sharp jagged teeth, nose scrunched, eyes narrowed, with a bone chilling growl coming from deep inside it's throat. Anyone could stand outside the beasts cage, point to it and say, "I'm not afraid of that." It takes a special human being, a special athlete, to position themselves on all fours, get inside the cage with that dog, and while staring the wild animal in the face say with conviction, "I am not afraid of you." _That_ is having the courage to fail. _That_ is where excitement stems from.

Sometimes, on the day of a game that carries more importance, a game in which failing would hurt worse than others, nervousness might creep into the body, it might try to find a home and manifest in the stomach. As I rode the elevator and saw my family, both my biological one and my softball one, I knew right away the type of butterflies that were forming within me. Because of those people in the lobby, I had the courage and the strength to stare this animal in the face. I was filled with an excitement not comparable to anything else in my life. I could not wait to march into battle with my team that night.

CHAPTER 2

"THE SOONER YOU REALIZE IT'S NOT ALL ABOUT YOU, THE BETTER OFF YOU'LL BE."

E very August, preseason starts off with the first team meeting of the year. This was something that I would really look forward to. During the regular season you go from seeing your teammates, coaches, and trainers every single day to not seeing them at all for the two months of summer. If you are a part of a team that truly cares about one another and enjoys each others' company, then the first meeting of the year feels like a long anticipated family reunion.

The first team meeting my freshman year was one of my favorites. The Alabama softball team had just come off a successful season where they had finished third in the WCWS. They had received quite a bit of screen time in which Bama legends like Brittany Rogers, Kelley Montalvo, Ashley Holcombe, and Charlotte Morgan truly shined in the spotlight. It started to sink in that *I* was teammates with *them*. Honestly, I was star-struck at that first meeting. I shied away in the corner in hope that no one would speak to me. However, as I know now, Alabama softball players are programmed to welcome the scared, quiet freshman hovered in the corner. In my feeble attempt to camouflage into the wall, I actually made myself the most obvious target. Everyone put in extra effort to try and make me feel welcomed.

Each of the coaches said their piece at that meeting. I learned a lot from listening to them speak. Your first time doing anything you can either choose to be overwhelmed by the experience or you can choose to be a sponge that absorbs and retains as much as you can. In that meeting, it didn't take long for us to get hit with advice that would change our lives. Coach Murphy looked at every single one of the incoming freshmen and said, "I'm going to tell the five of you what I tell every other freshman class when they first arrive on campus."

'Here it is.' I excitedly thought to myself. The restricted file, the message that is going to be the key to unlocking any worry or uncertainty I have as a freshman. I was about to get slammed right in the face with the secret to success. Coach Murphy with a straight face said very calmly yet sternly, "The sooner you realize it is not all about you, the better off you're going to be."

Think about that for a second. Picture being a freshman. You were one of the most highly recruited softball players in the nation. Whatever team you just came from, *you* were the best of the best. You were it. You were written about in the local paper, and your parents, family members, and friends all made a big deal about you going to *the* University of Alabama to play softball. Then the very first thing you hear is, guess what, this is not all about you.

For some players this can be a very difficult concept to grasp. There are anywhere from 17-20 players on a team and only nine of them get to play at one time. That means you have a lot of players sitting on the bench. If you play for a successful program, then all of the 'bench players' consist of former MVP's, All-State Honorees, and Gatorade Player of Year recipients. They are not used to sitting and they are not accustomed to having to watch someone else play 'their' position. While getting recruited by the University of Alabama, we were not promised playing time. We were promised an opportunity to earn playing time and an opportunity to be a part of an extraordinary team.

On a team, the ability for the non-starters to grasp this concept is just as important for those who are starting. If your name is written down on the lineup card for that day, or your name is called to pinch hit later in the game, you better be thankful for the opportunity either way. That really is what life is all about: Being grateful for the opportunities that are presented to you and trying to make the most of them.

The underlying message throughout the Alabama Softball program was that it is never about you. What about when you are offered a scholarship? Not about you. When you show up to your first practice? Not about you. When you hit your first homerun? Not about you. When you strikeout for the third time in one game? Still not about you. Well, if it's not about you, then who is it about?

My freshman year I was sitting in my dorm talking on the phone with a former coach of mine. During that conversation, she mentioned her difficulty sharing an office space with a co-worker who was applying for the same head coaching position as her. "Cassie, imagine that a lefty hitter, lefty fielder who played first base and outfield, just like you, was your roommate. Wouldn't that be difficult?" She explained. I quickly replied and agreed that a situation like that would indeed by tough to handle.

Just then my roommate, Jazlyn Lunceford passed by my door and reminded me the rest of the freshman class would be heading to dinner soon.

And it suddenly hit me. Jazlyn Lunceford, fellow freshman… lefty hitter…lefty fielder…played first base and outfield in high school.

No… How did I not recognize this sooner? I started laughing and explained my sudden realization to my coach on the phone. She too had to laugh at my shocking realization.

I still find it funny that I never recognized the correlation between Jaz and I as roommates. Did our coaches realize this? Did they room us together on purpose? I asked Jaz later on if she had realized our interesting living situation. She had not, but she too found it comical that it had taken us over half a semester to see it.

Whatever the reasoning was, I'm very thankful we ended up that first year as roommates. Jaz and I are still great friends to this day. We have always cheered for each other. We've always had an understanding that we would fight and push each other to better ourselves. No matter who ended up starting that day, we had an understanding that it wasn't because one of us was playing worse than the other. It was because one of us was hitting our stride at the right time and would benefit the team that day. We would pick each other up and help each other through our struggles because honestly, who better to do so than someone in the same position? They are literally in your shoes on the field when you're not.

I have a difficult question for you. Do you hate to fail? Or do you hate to lose? It has become an unfortunate theme in the sport of softball that younger players seem to hate to fail yet they don't know how to hate to lose. *Hating to fail* is a concept that directs the focus on you. *Hating to fail* means getting upset when you strikeout or make an error. Not because it hurt the team, but because it made you look bad. However, *hating to lose* is a completely different animal. *Hating to lose* puts the focus on your team. It emphasizes the name on the front of your jersey and not the one on the back. *Hating to lose* lights a fire beneath you and enables your motivation to outwork and outfight any opponent. *Hating to lose* brings tears of frustration and anger to your eyes as you watch another team celebrate a victory on your field. Those who *hate to lose* won't laugh on the bus ride home five minutes after a loss. Those who *hate to lose* will dread waking up the morning following a loss because they'll know the loss will be the very first thing that comes to their mind. *Hating to lose* makes it all about the team and brings fourth the best traits of competitiveness. *Hating to fail* leads to a shrug of the shoulders after a loss. It causes players to feel above the team as if their struggles are suddenly more significant than any one else's. It's as if their success is more important than the wins and loss record. *Hating to fail* will lead you to play for an All-American accolade. *Hating to lose* will lead you to hoisting a national championship trophy.

The title of this chapter could have just as easily been the title for this book. It is a common thread that runs deep throughout the Alabama Softball program. It has been a staple and an overarching principle that has held individuals accountable, pushed players to their limit, and above all, bound us together as a family. It is constantly referenced and because every person from the coaches, support staff, seniors, and freshman wholeheartedly embraced this, we found success. Even in the years we didn't win our last game, we were successful because we lived by this creed. We understood it would take everyone, not just an individual, to win it all.

I absolutely loved playing games at night. There was something so special about night games. I think there are a number of reasons for this. As a kid, there were only a few special times that we had the opportunity to play after dark, not many little league fields even had lights available. Nighttime always signified an end to the fun and an end to the games. Once the streetlights flickered on, that was our cue to head inside. But those lights that towered over the softball diamond, they were our extra life, our cheat code to keep playing longer. Night games filled us with anticipation and excitement not just because we got to play past dark, but also because every championship game that is ever played, is done so under the lights. No world series was ever won at 1pm when the sun was shining. No, we grew up huddled in front of the television staring wide-eyed at our heroes celebrating like children at night, under the lights.

The anticipation for a night game kills me. Waiting around in a hotel room all day can be considered a form of torture. I came from our team lunch and laid down on my bed. I closed my eyes and started to picture the game that night. I truly feel that any successful player or team visualizes their success hundreds of times before it ever happens. Although visualizing doesn't guarantee success on the field, I strongly believe it gives you the best chance to succeed, especially when the stakes are highest.

I would try and set aside at least thirty minutes before every game to do this. Like a physical skill, the mental game gets better with practice. By the end of the season I was able to put myself in a game situation with such detail that my visions contained the vividness of a video recording instead of the fogginess associated with a dream.

With as much detail as possible I pictured lacing up my cleats and walking out onto that field. I imagined hearing the noise my metal spikes would make as they came into contact with dirt, what the crowd would sound like, what the air would feel like. I pictured putting my batting gloves and helmet on, selecting my bat and walking up to the batter's box. I tried to feel my routine in my head. The better I could predict my potential nerves now during visualizing, the greater my mental advantage would be in the game.

Beneath my closed eyelids I began to paint a picture of what the stadium would look like that night. Everything from the tint of the green grass to the crimson and white of our jerseys jumped to life in my mind. My senses gave way to the dream-like state I drifted into. Almost instantly my body emulated the nerves I would eventually feel as I felt myself stepping off the top step of the dugout and walking toward home plate for my first at-bat. I took advantage of calming these nerves and practicing my swing thought over and over again, "See it big. Slow it down. I will crush this pitch." As if I were watching re-runs from a television show, I clearly saw each of my previous at-bats against Oklahoma's pitcher from the first two games of the series. Like a conductor, I controlled the characters of my visualization and demanded success in every move I made. I imagined swinging at pitches thrown into my hitting zone and taking those that just missed the infamous black outline of home plate. I envisioned every possible defensive scenario that I may encounter. Inning by inning I outlined the entire game in my mind and like a fine-tuned orchestra, my teammates were triumphant in every aspect. By the time I choreographed the whole game, up to the very last out, I felt calm, confident, and in complete control of my emotions.

Suddenly, I felt my phone vibrate.

"Text message: Nick Seiler." Appeared on the screen.

I was expecting the text from our athletic trainer to read, "Ankle taping beginning at 4:00pm," just like every other day.

Instead it said, "Valley toss. Hallway, now."

I jumped out of bed. "Ryan!"

"I know! I know! I got the text, too. Getting my shoes on now!"
She responded from the other room. As we ran out the door we felt like
kids again, giddy with excitement.

Our teammates were already taking their positions in the hotel
for the event that was about to occur: The Valley Toss. Before fully
understanding this game, you will have to know the set up of our hotel.
We were staying at an Embassy Suites. All of the rooms were positioned
on the perimeter of the hotel, leaving an open rectangle in the middle
that all the hallways on each floor overlooked. In the middle of this large
rectangle was the lobby, a seating area, two elevators, and finally on the
other side of the elevators, the hotel's dining space. The length of this
hotel was about half the size of a football field. Our beloved athletic
trainer, Nick had the idea of the century that saved the day for our team.

Twenty-four hours earlier, Nick attempted a 'Valley Toss' by
throwing his Frisbee the entire length of the hotel courtyard. From the
fourth floor hallway Nick would have to throw the Frisbee over 50
yards, making it over the lobby and seating area below, through the
skinny passageway between the two elevators, over the dining room and
finally into the hands of a teammate on the other end of the hotel. We
had people positioned on every floor at all areas, strategically set up to
retrieve an errant thrown Frisbee and return it to the 'tosser' as quickly
as possible. If a Frisbee ricocheted off of the elevator and into the dining
area, we would need someone to throw the Frisbee from the dining area
to the first floor, to the second floor, followed by the third floor, finally
reaching the 'tosser' on the fourth floor. Getting the Frisbee from the
ground floor back to the 'tosser' was almost as big of an accomplishment
as completing the actual 'Valley Toss.'

Twenty girls sitting in a hotel room anxiously awaiting the biggest
game of their lives creates an exhaustive excitement. It was so important
for Nick to give us that vice to have fun. For that afternoon we were able

to forget about the enormity of the impending game. During the 'Valley Toss' we cheered and laughed and acted like we were the only people in that hotel. We even had the hotel workers and fellow guests encouraging us and helping get the Frisbees back to the 'tossers.' Whenever we did complete the 'Valley toss,' we celebrated as if someone had just hit a homerun. We were having a blast. We were enjoying each other's company. Depending on how the game would go later that night, these could have been our last celebrations together.

I think that's why people were attracted to us. So many fans from all over the country showed their support for our program. We did everything with a child-like excitement, including playing the game of softball. Being able to compete in the final softball game of your life, and still play it with your best friends as if you were ten years old in the backyard would be what would help us in the game that night. I believe with everything I have that playing this game with the kind of passion, love, and energy of a kid is when softball is played at it's best. The only difference about the game we were about to play tonight and the one we played when we were ten is that when the lights came on, it didn't mean game-over, it meant the fun was just about to start.

CHAPTER 3

"TRADITION NEVER GRADUATES"

On game day, when you see your name absent from the starting lineup you have two options. You can choose to make it all about you and sulk in the dugout, barely cheering and feeling down and out. Or the alternative is to find a way to contribute in a positive way. Understanding that it is always your job to find a way to help the team in anyway possible in pertinent to success. Contributions can came from encouraging a teammate when they are struggling, decoding the opposing teams signs and signals, or discovering a pattern in the way the pitcher is throwing. Even the smallest of details can be pivotal. As a team member, you have the potential to help the offense out without ever stepping foot into the batter's box. Thinking that you cannot contribute is the furthest thing from the truth.

The best example of this is former outfielder, Jessica Smith. Jess showed up to the University of Alabama as the reigning high school record holder for homeruns in the state of Alabama. She was a strong catcher with a cannon for an arm and was eager to have a chance to go to one of the best universities in her home state. Unfortunately, on the first day of spring practice her freshman year while completing a warm-up drill, Jess tore the ACL in her right knee. Devastated, she had to red-shirt and sit out her first year of competition. For the next nine months Jess worked as hard as ever to get back onto the field healthy again. During that time period she began to have shoulder issues, only to find out she had torn the labrum of her throwing arm.

Finally, after both surgeries, Jess was cleared to train with the team again. The very first test of her newly repaired knee was a conditioning session at Alabama's indoor turf facility. While running sprints, Jess accidentally stepped on a teammates foot and collapsed holding her knee. She said she felt no pain but instantly began to sob. The noise of a towel ripping in half echoed as Jess fell to the ground. She knew right away the all too familiar feeling. Although, this was not her right knee that had just been repaired, this was her 'healthy' knee. Just four short months after her shoulder surgery, Jess's left knee now had a torn MCL, ACL, and meniscus.

Anyone who has experienced a knee injury knows that Jess' primary position of catching would now be her secondary, or tertiary, position. She would now for the most part be an outfielder full-time. Still, she soldiered forward completing countless hours of rehabilitation work.

Take a second to pause and imagine this. You are recruited from your home state of Alabama to play at *the* University of Alabama. All of your friends and family are cheering you on to succeed and you aren't even healthy enough to play, plagued by one devastating injury after another. Your knees are shot and you can no longer catch. Your arm that was once a cannon is now surgically repaired and will never be what it used to be. It sounds like a textbook reason for someone to complain, doesn't it? I wouldn't blame her if she did complain; she was spending three hours a day in the rehab facility and for what? She wasn't an everyday starter, she had a hard time proving herself in practice because her body no longer worked the way it was supposed to. This was undoubtedly a difficult time for Jess, as it would be for any competitive athlete.

You may be asking, "So, where's the happy ending," right? In the stats books, Jessica Smith ended her senior year only starting four games. But, she finished that year with over 1,500 at-bats. You see, instead of sitting on the bench every game of her career and cursing the skies for her bad luck, she turned her struggles into a positive for the team. Why? Because she knew it wasn't about her. Nothing good could come out of her sitting the bench dwelling on the bad hand she had been dealt.

Jess became well known throughout the SEC and a constant headache for opposing pitching coaches. A rival head coach once walked by our dugout and in a joking manner said, "Ugh! You're still here?! I thought you graduated!" Only four starts but over 1,500 at-bats? Impossible, right? Not quite.

Jess was our spy, and a good one, too. She had a binder filled to the brim, six inches thick with charts. Every game, Jess with her iconic clipboard would take her spot on the first step of our dugout and with her glasses on, she'd stare at the pitching coach in the opposite dugout. She would chart every movement they made knowing that even a scratch of the head could be a potential sign for a change-up. Her eyes would shift from the pitching coach to the catcher. The catcher's set up, the way she leaned, her body language, how she would smack her glove before the incoming pitch. All of these things were vital pieces to solving an intricate puzzle and her expertise as a catcher certainly came into play. Each game, Jess' voice would be with us during every at-bat. We had a set of cue words to indicate pitch type and location. I can't tell you how many at-bats we had where we knew exactly what pitch was coming before the pitcher even started her motion. Can you fathom how much easier an at-bat is when you as a hitter know what the pitch is going to be? Can you imagine how frustrating that is to a pitcher? Do you know how many homeruns, triples, doubles, and RBI's Jessica Smith was responsible for? The numbers would be endless, too many to count.

Jessica Smith was our unsung hero. Day in and day out she'd pick up her binder from her top compartment in her locker, grimacing from the overhead weight on her sore surgically repaired shoulder. She'd search through the papers collecting any charts she could use from games played against this particular team in the past. Then she'd slowly make her way to the field, gingerly walk down the stairs into the dugout, hobbling on the last step as to avoid bending her knee. Then, she'd finally find her 'spot' in the dugout. She had to be in perfect view of the opposing teams dugout, all the while concealed from plain sight. With her glasses on, she was an undercover detail hidden in the intertwined fabric of this game. To an outsider, no one would ever know what her job was but to us, she was the epitome of a selfless teammate. Someone who made it all about her teammates and never about herself. She got it. And because she got it, her picture now resides on the left field wall alongside other Alabama Softball legends, typically reserved for All-Americans.

Jessica Smith's last year of eligibility with the Alabama Softball program was 2010. Although she was not physically with us in 2012, the legacy that she left will always be with that program. Jess gave us the blueprint of a selfless, 'we before me' attitude that will always be engrained at Alabama. Her binder has been passed down from player to player throughout the years after her graduation. The reason Alabama Softball was successful in 2012 was not just because of the players on the current team, but all those players that had come before. Each one laying the foundations on which future championship contending teams could be built. Every team carries a footprint of players that came before them. When current Alabama teams are successful, I believe each member of the Bama softball family, past, present, and future, walks a little taller and a little prouder because of it.

To show us the importance of character and instill values, our coaches would always find the best videos to show us. One video in particular taught us the true meaning of "tradition never graduates" and what it means to leave a legacy. It was Tom Rinaldi's ESPN story about Welles Crowther's red bandana. When Welles was a young boy, his father gave him a red bandana. For the rest of his life he would carry that bandana around everywhere he went. It became his signature. Welles went on to become a Division I lacrosse player at Boston College. After college he got a job working at the World Trade Center in New York City. Unfortunately, during the tragic attacks that took place on September 11, 2001, Welles Crowther's life was taken. In the weeks and months that followed this tragedy, his heartbroken parents searched the newspapers, reading every painful story and interview published to see if they could find a glimpse of their son's final moments. Finally, they found him. On several accounts, survivors told a story of a man that appeared out of nowhere to help the injured victims. In each account, this man wore a red bandana. The man helped people down the stairs, put out fires, and tended to those who were wounded. These stories spoke of the man with the red bandana leading survivors to safety down the stairs only to turn back into the chaos, running to find more in need of help.

It is believed that Welles Crowther saved as many as twelve peoples lives before the South Tower collapsed at 9:59 am. Now over twelve years later, Welles is remembered throughout the country for his bravery. Every fall, New England hosts a red bandana run. In 2006 he was named an honorary New York City firefighter and revered as 'a true hero.' One of his former teammates reflects on Welles and states, "For me, the red bandana symbolizes everything I want to be and everything that Welles was; strength, honor, courage." Tom Rinaldi ends the story with the narrator asking the audience, "What would you do in the last hour of your life? What would it look like? Would it be the thread of legacy and the color of honor?"

After the video was completed, I don't believe there was a dry eye amongst our team in that meeting room. Coach Murphy looked at all of us and said, "Look at the legacy he left behind." It truly was incredible. Here is a man who embraced the meaning of selflessness. He didn't even know these people, yet when chaos erupted he was thinking about everyone but himself. He put the safety of others before his own. He was a true servant leader. Murphy then looked at all the seniors and said, "So, what's it going to be? What will your legacy be when you leave here? What are they going to be saying about you?"

The very next day we walked into the locker room to find six red bandanas hanging from each of the seniors' lockers. That bandana meant so much more to us than any Nike apparel or Easton equipment we had been given throughout the years. That red bandana represented a responsibility to make anything that we were a part of better in some way. Our coaches had tasked us to write a long lasting legacy in the story that is Alabama Softball. We had been a part of three chapters from our freshman to junior years and now we had the pen. We had the opportunity to write our final chapter. What were they going to say about us when we walked out of this place?

It was finally time to get dressed and ready to leave for the game. I put my sliding shorts on, followed by my white pants. I only had one sock on as my right bare foot would need taping soon. Every time I did something, I thought, "This is your last time getting ready for a game, last time getting dressed in this uniform, last time getting taped." Although all of these thoughts crossed my mind, none of them really hit me. There was no significant feeling associated with any of these thoughts and I am so thankful for that. I think those feelings would have been too overwhelming to deal with at the time. There was something more important that required my full emotional attention: The last game of the 2012 NCAA softball season, the last game of the championship series, the last game for myself and my fellow seniors in an Alabama uniform. How many athletes are so lucky to know when their last game will be no matter what? Win or lose we knew this would be it for us.

I walked upstairs to our trainer, Nick's hotel room. Inside the room music was playing, just like every other day. Tim and Ashley, our two student trainers, were busy tending to Kaila Hunt's toe taping and getting the bag packed for the game. My mind couldn't help but immediately think of Addy Hamilton.

Along with Tim and Ashley, Addy was our third student trainer for the spring of 2012. Addy was so much fun to be around. She always seemed to make her surrounding environment better with her lively personality. She was quick with a joke, always smiling, and willing to give so much of herself to make us better. On Wednesday, February 8, 2012 Addy experienced some concerning head pain at the end of our last practice before our first game of the season. On Thursday, we all texted and called her from our bus as we rode to Mobile, Alabama for our first tournament. She was in the hospital getting some tests run and still responded to our texts with something along the lines of, "Thanks yo! I love you guys! I got this fo sho! Don't worry about me!" Like I said, Addy had a very special personality that is reflected in that one text. Even during a time where she must've been filled with uncertainty and fear of the unknown, she got in the cage with fear, looked it in the eye and said, "I am not afraid of you." She showed us what true courage was all about.

On Friday, February 10, 2012 we won our first game of the season and immediately following the game, we were all sure to let Addy know the 'W' was for her and she needed to get better soon so she could join us next week. On Saturday, February 11 Addy was sent home from the hospital to get some rest before her scheduled surgery that Monday. On Sunday, February 12, we won our fourth and final game of the tournament. In the huddle afterwards Coach Murphy looked at all of us and said, "I want you all to know how much you mean to me and that I love every single one of you very much." This was a different post game speech than we were used to hearing. Freshman Danielle Richard had just hit her first collegiate homerun and junior Keima Davis had a clutch hit as well. I thought those plays from the game would be highlighted in our post game meeting. Then, Nick stepped forward in the huddle, his lips were tight as the words fell out of his mouth, "Addy passed away last night."

I felt my eyes instantly water and my throat tighten. I was in shock. Her surgery was tomorrow, we just talked to her yesterday, we just saw her on Wednesday, how could this be? I felt my teammate Danae's head fall on my shoulder from behind. She was sobbing, we all were. I grabbed her arm and told her it would be okay, even though I felt the furthest thing from okay. I felt like someone had punched me in the stomach. I couldn't comprehend this loss.

Nobody can control where they are at a time of devastating news. I was never more thankful than to be surrounded by my team. Many said that Addy was our angel in the outfield the rest of the season and I couldn't help but notice, a lot of things went our way that year. I know Addy was with us, celebrating in the dugout, enjoying the season with the 2012 Alabama Softball team.

On June 6, 2012, the second I walked into Nick's room that day to get my foot taped, I knew she was there, too. She was with all of us.

Sometimes life hits you with a punch that hurts like no other. No matter the pain, there is always a value from every experience that we can take with us on the rest of our journey on Earth, despite how long or short it may be. It is hard not to have a newfound perspective and appreciation for life after a situation like this. For the rest of the season we would wear purple bracelet's with her initials and one simple quote that encompassed her personality all too well, "It's all good."

I noticed in our team and in the way we viewed a situation, that Addy in her short time with us was able to make a lasting impact and impression. One none of us will ever forget. Her strength in handling the situation like she did and having a positive attitude despite being in a hospital unsure of the cause of her symptoms was truly remarkable. How could our outlook on life not have been changed for the better? How could we ever be stressed about a bad test grade, upset when we struck out, or feel defeated when we were injured? How could we not view every situation that season with an, "It's all good" attitude? Thank you for teaching us that, Addy.

As I stood in the doorway of Nick's hotel room, thinking about Addy's energy for life I couldn't help but smile. "Cass! What's going on?" Nick said.

"Happy game-day!" I replied.

"Thoughts on tonight's game?" Tim asked from across the room.

"We got this." I calmly replied.

"Fo sho." Ashley chimed in.

I couldn't help but smile big again. Addy was in that room with us, there wasn't a doubt in my mind about it.

CHAPTER 4

"IF YOU HAVE SOMETHING NICE TO SAY, MAKE SURE YOU SAY IT."

Since we were young, we were taught that if we didn't have anything nice to say, then don't say anything at all. Well, what if you did you have something nice to say? It seems as a culture we have become uncomfortable with giving and receiving compliments. It's okay to tell the person next to you that you respect how hard they work at school. Or to tell your parents that you appreciate them and all they do for you. It's acceptable to tell your teammate that you admire their leadership abilities. It may feel awkward or uncomfortable in the moment but walking away after complimenting someone else will always leave both parties with a sentiment of gratitude.

Our program at Alabama was built around having an 'attitude of gratitude.' There were so many activities and games we would play throughout my career that put us all in a position to show our care and appreciation for one another. Here are just a few examples.

Affirmation Bag Week

Affirmation bag week was the week leading up to the first game of the season. The coaches would walk into our pre-practice meeting with brown bags and markers and we would get two minutes to decorate our bags with our name on them. It was always amusing how coloring would lead a bunch of mature, well-rounded college athletes to act like we were all five years old again.

Next, the coaches would explain that if you want a person to continue a certain behavior the two things you should do are model and affirm that behavior. If we wanted the freshman class to continue working extra on their own before and after practice, we as seniors needed to work extra ourselves and be sure to compliment a freshman when they came to the field to put in additional work.

Exactly one week before our first game of the season, we would line all of our brown paper bags on the windowsill of the clubhouse. Throughout the week we would write on little pieces of scrap paper an affirmation for one of our teammates and place it into their bag. It could be a physical affirmation: "Your backhands are improving everyday! Keep up the great work at second base, you can really tell it's paying off." Or maybe a character affirmation: "I am so thankful to have had the opportunity to get to know you off the field, you are such a strong person and I really look up to you for how you have handled adversity".

The affirmations could be long or short, anonymous or signed and about a number of different things. The bottom line was that by the end of the week you would have an affirmation from every player, coach, trainer, manager, and support staff in the program and they would all have at least one from you. After going home and reading all the great things the people surrounding you everyday had to say about you, it made you feel pretty good, and it was just in time for our first game. Long time softball coach Mike Candrea from the University of Arizona once said, "Boys have to play good to feel good, but girls have to feel good to play good." If our team was feeling good about themselves leading up to a game, it was usually a good indication that we'd play well. Reading over those affirmations still to this day can turn any bad day around into a better one for me.

The Huddle

The end of practice huddle was another tool we used to express our thoughts about each other. Every once in a while at the very end of practice, the coaches would call us into a final huddle before we would be dismissed. We would briefly go over key moments that needed to be addressed from practice, what people did well, and what we still needed to work on in order to continue to get better. Once that was settled, we would sometimes get to play a little game. Murphy would clap his hands together and say, "Okay!" as he exhaled with excitement. He would then recite the rules of the 'game' for that day.

Some practices we would turn to the person to our right and tell them something that they have done really well. Other days we would turn to the person to our left and tell them something we now know about them this year that we didn't know about them the year before. Every time we did this, there was a different rule added. One time, the person to our right told us something that we had to get better at. Then in return we had to give them a compliment about something they did really well. Not too many female teams are able to receive a criticism and then return with a compliment. It takes a special group of girls that completely trust one another's perspectives in order to do this.

I really liked those exercises. I especially liked hearing from people on the team that wouldn't normally speak up in a huddle. There are so many different perspectives a team or a sport can be viewed from. Seeing what one teammate was able to pick up on and see in others told all of us a little something about that player's values. These were the people we were going to be surrounded by the most. They were the ones we ate with, traveled with, worked out with, went to class with, lived with and most importantly played with. Having a bond with your teammates off the field that can translate and contribute to success on the field is rare. These huddles always seemed to enhance those bonds.

There is something special about being in a huddle. There is a reason a huddle is not square or triangular. A huddle is round so that all members can clearly see one another and hear each other when they speak. In a huddle there is no person better than the next, no person is sitting or kneeling as a coach stands and speaks down to him or her. The team is united, facing inward, managing their focus on the most important thing to them, their teammates. I can still remember the last huddle I was ever a part of. I realized it only at the end, when all of our hands were pointed toward the middle joining us as one. I took a step back in my mind for only a second, and in that instance got chills that traveled throughout my whole body. I believe your mind knows when you are a part of a once in a lifetime rarity. I believe the mind restricts you only a short glimpse of this feeling. Any longer than that would be too overwhelming. The next time you see a team standing in a huddle together, holding each others backs, ask yourself this question: When was the last time you had someone in your life who you knew, without an ounce of doubt, had your back no matter what? Someone that you could rely on regardless of the circumstance and who would fight with you to accomplish your goals and dreams. Now, imagine what it would feel like to have *nineteen* people willing to do that for you. Picture the immense, overwhelming feeling that would rush over you whenever you were surrounded by these individuals. That is a team. That is what makes it so special.

I Have Your Back

Another favorite was the, 'I have your back' game. The coaches would explain to us that as a team, we were a family and no matter what we would have each other's back. Our coaches instilled in us that each person on our team brings something unique and special to the table. Everyone would have a blank piece of paper taped to their back and we would all get a pen. For the next thirty minutes we would spend time walking around writing on each persons back what we thought they brought to the table daily that we appreciated about them. After everyone had a comment from each other we'd all sit in a circle and read the comments out loud. We would then have to guess and try and figure out which class member or coach wrote that on our back. Once the author was discovered we would look them in the eyes and say, "Thank you" with sincerity. I still have that paper that was taped to my back and it is packed with my teammates and coaches handwriting and compliments. I don't think it will ever lose its power of making my day.

Actually verbalizing your words out loud when you have something nice to say is important. Providing an environment for people who may be too shy to say so on their own is even better. What I've found from being on a team my entire life is that those who are hesitant to say much on their own usually are the ones that have the best things to say.

Sophomore, Kaila Hunt was a great example of this. She was very soft spoken when she first showed up at Alabama. Loud vocals and pre-game motivational speeches were not Kaila's style. Instead she brought a presence that screamed volumes. I had the honor to bat in the line-up right before her a couple of times throughout my career. Any time I didn't get the job done, as I jogged back to the dugout she'd look at me and go, "Hey, I got your back." She didn't have to yell it so everyone on the team, the coaches, or the stands heard it. All she had to do was convey it to me. She took away any frustration or disappointment I had and took the responsibility of getting the job done and put it on herself.

Someone recently asked me if I liked getting 'high-fived' from a teammate after I struck out. I'm not sure anyone does. It's like a dog getting a treat after not performing the trick. Of course the person offering the high-five is only trying to provide comfort and support to their teammate. Unfortunately, they usually end up on the wrong end of the hitter's bad mood. I think the best thing you can say to someone who has just failed at their job whatever it may be is, "Hey, she's got your back right here" or "We're going to pick you up." That weight of failure doesn't seem so heavy when you have teammates who express their support like that.

Bucket Filler

We had a concept on our team about filling buckets. Every person has his or her own metaphorical bucket and shovel. When you would compliment or share a positive affirmation with someone, both you and the recipient added a scoop to your buckets. That mutual positive interaction makes both parties feel good. However, when you speak poorly about someone or criticize them in a negative way, not only do you take a scoop out of their bucket, but you take a scoop out of yours as well.

Challenge yourself to fill a different person's bucket each day. The challenge lies not in simply providing others with compliments and praise, but doing so absent of selfish desires. Be motivated to encourage others just for the sake of enriching another person's life. If you do this, by day's end you will be overwhelmed by how full your own heart will feel. Your overflowing bucket will be a byproduct of making someone's day just a little bit better.

Appreciating your teammate's roles on the team is a major aspect to achieving success on the field. Make sure you thank the catchers for taking a beating behind the plate and wearing the equipment even when it's hot out. Thank those who are injured for taking their rehab seriously and spending extra hours working to just get back on the field. Tell the battery you appreciate them for running extra before, during, and after practice. What about the dugout? All of those who are diligently working to find you an advantage while you are at the plate. The next time you slide into second base and pop up after a double off the wall, make sure you point to your dugout. Make sure you thank *them*, your team. It is because of *them* that you are successful. Do you know how far the statement, "Thank you, I appreciate what you do for this team" will go? When was the last time you thanked your teammates? Your coaches? Your parents? Vocalized your appreciation? Vocalized your compliments? No matter how uncomfortable it might be, it is always better to know that the people you love and care about in your life know how you feel about them.

When our student trainer, Addy Hamilton passed away in February of 2012, it was at the very end of our affirmation bag week. Coach Murphy made sure that she had her bag as she waited testing in the hospital. Addy passed away knowing exactly how we all felt about her. We articulated how much we appreciated her. How we loved the energy and spirit she brought to the table. How willing she was to give up so much of her time to help make us better. How thankful we were to have her a part of our family. Ask yourself if the people who surround your life everyday know exactly how you feel about them. If not, don't hesitate to tell them, it will probably make their day and in turn make your day better, too.

'Cleats, turfs, socks, pants, belt, spandex, batting practice top, uniform top, arm band, glove.' I repeated the checklist over and over again in my head as I walked to the bus. I had everything I needed physically, however my mental checklist may have been another story. As I got to the bus and grabbed the railing to pull myself up the steep steps another thought crept through my mind, "Last bus ride to a game." It was a hollow thought with no weight attached to it. Again, I was thankful these emotions waited to make their impact on me.

"Happy Gameday Cass!" My coaches Aly, Murphy, Steph VanBrakle, Adam Arbour (volunteer assistant), and Whitney Larsen (student assistant) all looked up at me from their seats in the front of the bus with a big smile. In that instant I knew that anything I was going to need was right here in front of me. We all got high fives from everyone the entire way to the back of the bus. Our support staff was such an integral part of our championship run. Skip Powers, our sports information director, his intern Nathan Kogut, and Chad Haynie, the voice of Alabama softball on the radio, were just as invested to this team as the people who were in the dugout during the game. Skip was dressed in his game-day outfit, the same outfit he wore every single game for good luck. Senior women's administrator, Marie Robbins, director or softball operations, Kate Harris, assistant director for games and events management, Ashley Waters, all awaited the team as we piled onto the bus one by one. You could tell in their emotion, their encouragement, and their passion that they wanted this for us in the worst way possible.

As I made my way down the isle I got nods, high-fives, and fist bumps from our strength and conditioning coach, Michelle Diltz, head trainer, Nick, the student trainers, Tim and Ashley and the one and only, Jim 'Doc' Laubenthal, our team doctor. It crossed my mind how many people on this team those core five had helped with injuries. None of us would have been healthy enough to play if it had not been for all of them. Today would mark our 68th game in a four-month span. If our bodies weren't healthy, our season would have probably ended fifteen games earlier. I heard Jason Nance, our equipment manager's deep voice say 'Roll Tide' quite a few times as I approached my seat in the back. Our beloved managers, Jordan Burson, Russell Larsen, Miles Snider, and Chandler Whidden, were just as fired up as we were. Being an only child I've never experienced a relationship with a sibling. However, I can imagine the way in which our managers cared about us and invested in us would be how it felt to have an older brother. I finally got to the seat of Scott Moyer and Christopher England, from TideTV, who were in charge of the video taping and editing for our team. They both worked tirelessly into the night, sacrificing sleep so that we could get the most up to date film of the pitcher and hitters we would be facing the next day. Each one of us would get our own DVD of the broken down game footage, an invaluable item during the World Series. They all bled Crimson and White, willing to give everything for this championship, willing to celebrate with us, make this happen for us, and do anything to win this title.

TideTV producer, Christopher England had a very special role on our team, one that would never get published in the papers or talked about on ESPN. However, the influence he had on our success was simply amazing. For every single game of the WCWS, Christopher would make highlights and motivational videos for us to watch on the way to the games. He was extremely talented in this regard. The reverence and enthusiasm Christopher had for the 2012 Alabama Softball team directly translated through these videos. His passion was imprinted onto us directly through the screen. As if it were contagious, within moments of watching his videos, the entire bus was plagued with an insatiable hunger for victory.

As I sat down in my seat I looked at my teammates and could not wipe the goofy smile off my face. We were all so excited for tonight's game. There was no fear, no doubt, and no insecurity in our hearts. We were ready for this game, we were about to play this game the way it was supposed to be played, with a child-like enjoyment coupled with the passion, fire, and determination of a starved animal hunting for food. We all leaned back in our chair and got ready for the video Christopher was about to reveal to us.

Bus rides to a game can vary depending on the team. Some prefer to be locked in with their headphones blaring focused on what they will have to do to perform. Some prefer silence so they can be in their own thoughts and mentally prepare themselves for competition. I have had some teammates that get overwhelmed if they incessantly think about the game. They find the need to talk to a teammate to avoid having paralysis by analysis set in. I'm not sure if anyone knew exactly what the best method was for a National Championship game televised on ESPN, but for us Christopher's videos worked. These videos showed us just how far we had come this season. At the same time they kept us focused on what was important now. The video kept us whole, engaged as a team opposed to compartmentalized in our own individual thoughts. The videos constantly affirmed how great we were by showing highlights of our top plays. Most importantly, the video provided blockades in our mind to protect against any creeping thoughts of doubt. It was a tool to help keep the poison out. The videos kept excitement high and nerves low.

The small television screens throughout our bus lit up with highlights of the game from the night before. Right away you could feel the excitement and the energy on the bus. This energy is a necessary component of competitiveness, yet one that cannot be measured. An intangible variable that requires no muscle from the weight room or skill from the practice field. This is a feeling that only those who have played on a team with so much passion and heart can understand. It was a feeling that I was fortunate enough to feel many times throughout my career at Alabama. It is a slow and steady beat that gains such momentum and continues with such ferocity that it teeters on becoming overwhelming. It is the feeling of twenty hearts beating in sync, beating as one. On that bus, there was nothing that could derail our momentum, nothing that could knock us off our tightrope.

Our team was locked in on the screens, engrossed with the game clips from the night before. Then came the motivational piece, the part that gave us goose bumps, filled our eyes with tears, and pumped our veins with adrenaline. It was as if I could feel my pupils dilating. Images of our team working out in the weight room, drenched with sweat, pushing our bodies to the max and then pushing even further. Clips from crucial points of our season were draped on the televisions, various motivational speeches from movies roared from the bus speakers. Matthew McConaughey from the movie, "We are Marshall" filled our ears and our hearts. "You gotta lay your heart on the line! If you do that, we cannot lose, we cannot be defeated!" I felt the chills creep across my legs. Morgan Freeman's voice boomed throughout our bus, "We sink, we swim, we rise, we fall, we meet our fate together!" Chills swept across my arms. "Live in the moment, cherish each moment! You're going to have to run and play all night!" The chills traveled to my neck. Finally one statement flashed on the screen. A statement that I knew in the instant I saw it would carry with us forever. The background music began to climb with anticipation, '20' appeared in white lettering on the black screen. The music boomed once again, still ascending with excitement, 'on' materialized on the monitor next. Finally, as the last crescendo of the music blasted, 'one' flashed across the screen completing the infamous statement: '20 on one.'

'20 on one.' The chills had traveled to the cheeks on my face and I couldn't help my eyes from filling with tears. I felt Amanda Locke

44

in the seat next tightly squeeze my right arm. I knew in that instant I wasn't the only one who felt 'it.' This was a feeling that we could not measure. It wasn't the velocity of a pitcher's pitch, or the distance of a homerun hit, or the range of an infielders ability. No, this was so much more, this was our heart. And on that bus ride on the way to the last game of our season, our hearts had swelled to an immeasurable size. They were full.

We watched that video on repeat three times before we finally arrived at ASA Hall of Fame Stadium. ESPN reporter Holly Rowe got on the bus with us. She had been working overtime to get the behind the scenes stories on the teams competing to report during the game. You could tell that she was in love with her job and truly enjoyed being there. Our team was beyond fired up for this game, we were ready, we were prepared to do this and to finally bring home a national championship for the University of Alabama.

We got off the bus with an extra bounce in our step. After having to wait all day for game time we would finally be able to warm up and let some of this excited energy out. As I walked into the locker room our team was loud! I loved how fired up we were. We were high fiving, cheering, and chanting. We were so eager for our time to play, our chance to compete, our opportunity to make our dream become a living reality!

"Get out your phones and call your parents." Coach Murphy walked in and silenced the locker room. This was a rather odd request from our coach. Everyone's phones had been turned off before even getting on the bus and no one was prepared to make any calls again until after the game. "Tell your parents to not come into the stadium yet. We're in a rain delay…and it's going to be a while." The locker room that echoed with excitement only moment's prior was now dead silent.

Rain. Something we had absolutely no control over. As a team we had a couple of options during this rain delay. We could sit and worry and make ourselves anxious over the unknown and the uncontrollable.

'When will the rain pass? When will we start playing tonight? Will we play tonight at all?' I didn't want to have to fall asleep, wake up, and do this whole day over again. I didn't want to break our momentum from the night before. This was the biggest game in any of our softball careers. We wanted to play. We wanted to win. And we wanted it to happen tonight.

Our second option was to enjoy each other's company. Over the course of the next two hours we did just that. We had just enough fun to distract ourselves. Just enough to keep the poison from creeping in, but not too much as to lose focus on the game. This was a crucial time for us. Mental exhaustion was a serious threat at this point. The intensity of the games, the pressure that came with the magnitude of this series, the cumulative weight that continues to mount throughout the week can be exponentially more wearing than any physical demand. Instead, we traded our anxiety for child like excitement. We focused our attention to the pureness of the game and it forced the doubts and insecurities out of the locker room.

So we waited. And waited. Then waited some more.

We had the entire team including coaches and support staff in that locker room together. It had a comfortable feel to it, just like being at home surrounded by family would. We did a number of things to stay entertained. Anything from playing cards, tweezing eyebrows, coming up with cheerleading routines, even power napping. Coach Aly joked that the rain delay was just extending the senior's time as a member of the Crimson Tide softball team. Aly always had a way of putting a positive spin on any situation.

Thankfully for myself and Dr. Laubenthal (who were die-hard Yankee fans) and not so much for Coach Murphy (a diehard anti-Yankees fan) there was one television in the locker room that was stuck on ESPN, which at the time was airing the Yankees game. Doc made a comment about how there was something special about the Yankees *being on T.V. during a time like this. He felt the fact that they were winning was a good sign for our game tonight. I couldn't help but smile and agree. Watching the most successful team in baseball history right before you and your team had a chance to make history was just another way to keep the poison from creeping in during that rain delay.*

Frequently throughout the rain delay we would get visits from ESPN's Holly Rowe. No matter how busy she was she always had a smile on her face. Here was an ESPN reporter that covered major sporting events at the professional and collegiate level all across the country. Yet, she was able to remember tiny details about each player. She was able to make you feel comfortable and make you feel important. I asked her if she knew a best-case scenario and worst-case scenario for tonight's game with the rain delay.

"Well, it looks like best-case scenario is we will start this game before 11:00 pm tonight. Worst-case scenario, we may play the game at a different field that didn't get as much rain. Or, we will play tomorrow afternoon or night." Holly replied.

I hated to think about not playing tonight. It gave way to a swell of anxiety and nerves that I wasn't sure my mental defenses were prepared to hold off any longer. 'Stay in the present, control what you can control.' I pounded this thought into my mind over and over again. I knew if we had to, we would do what we needed to do to win it all. I just believed we were all so ready. The next time we went to sleep we wanted it to be as national champions.

With that Murph walked into the locker room.

"Hey. Everyone over here." He said. The locker room quickly fell silent, all eyes, all of our attention, were locked in on him.

"We just met with the NCAA and here's what's going to happen for tonight..."

Chapter 5

"20 on One."

P rior to game three of the national championship game, Coach Alyson Habetz's voice boomed, "No matter what you do tonight, you are not doing it alone, you have all of us with you, you understand that? We are doing this thing together!" Her words hit all of us head on. The messages of her pre-game speech were inspiring enough to reach to the depths of our core. Some people said it was because she was good with choosing her words or that she would practice her speeches prior to the huddle. There were so many theories as to how she could get us every time to lock in on her every word. My theory was that she had her finger directly on the pulse of this team. She knew exactly what we needed to hear before we did. She had that motherly instinct and wanted to do anything in her power to see us succeed. She saw our team winning this championship and she wanted it more than anything for us.

"It's 20 on one the whole night, and nobody..." a smile crept across Aly's face as she made eye contact with each and every one of us, "I mean *nobody* can take on all 20 of you."

For that series and for that one night, our team developed this idea centered around 20 on one. No matter the situation, everything we did that night we were going to have the whole team with us. Imagine stepping in the batter's box and your team was behind you prepared to go to battle? Picture standing on the pitcher's mound and the entire team was with you in the circle? With 20 on one odds, I'd say a pretty strong feeling of invincibility would manifest.

This 20 on one mindset helped the most in times of adversity and during times of increased pressure. "Hey, we're going to pick you up right here, don't worry about it, we've got your back." That one statement could go a mile for a teammate struggling. Now, in addition to instilling invincibility, '20 on one' would provide a blanket of comfort. Our team embraced this idea and ran with it.

When walking to the plate, the ground shook with every step for it was 20 feet landing as one. Every swing we took was with the velocity of 20 bats. Every pitch thrown was with the intensity of 20 wind-ups. No matter how high the mountain seemed, we knew we could reach the summit together.

This idea of 'us' versus 'you' was so much more than that pre-game pep talk. It was something we had to feel, and with such a strong feeling came extraordinary actions. Passion oozed from the walls of our dugout, every teammate was locked in on every pitch. We were right there in the moment for our teammate in action. We were able to lose ourselves in a celebration for one another. Whether it was a foul tip, a borderline pitch taken for a ball, or a successfully fielded routine ground ball, we were able to recognize and therefore celebrate every little thing because in a way, that was *us* fielding that ball too. We were invested, committed, and we felt unstoppable with each of our teammates by our side.

Proof of this long-term commitment to 20 on one came sooner than expected for me. After my career was all said and done, I returned to Tuscaloosa, Alabama to move out of my apartment. The new changes in my life were officially setting in. I kept thinking over and over again about something I had heard three years earlier as a freshman. When my first year with the program ended, I asked senior Kelley Montalvo what she was going to miss most about Alabama softball. She replied, "It's having the girls and having that family atmosphere. For four years I knew for sure that I could rely on my team and they would have my back no matter what. I just don't know if I'm going to have that in the real world once I leave here."

This statement circled over and over again in my mind in the months leading up to as well as the months following my last game with the team. I knew I had friends for life in my former teammates, but I didn't have a team anymore. I no longer woke up feeling a part of team and that got to me, it kept eating away at me. Jordan Patterson was my teammate for the 2011 and 2012 seasons. Her mother had been the gymnastics coach at the University of Alabama for 34 years at the time and had seen a lot of success in her coaching career. One of my favorite parts about walking around coach Sarah Patterson's office was seeing the pictures she had of her former players. Pictures of their wedding days and children, so many of her athletes going on to live happy lives after their athletic careers were a thing of the past.

Exactly seventeen days following the national championship game, I found myself back in Tuscaloosa. The Patrick Murphy annual softball camp had just concluded and players past and present went out to eat at a local restaurant together. Jordan

Patterson sat down next to me as we waited to get seated and she asked how I was doing. I can remember our conversation as if it happened yesterday.

"I think it's really starting to set in that I'm not playing for Alabama anymore." I told her. "I'm having a hard time realizing I'm not a part of a team anymore, Jo. It is such a weird feeling, I've never *not* had a team."

What Jordan said next will stick with me for the rest of my life. "Cassie, I've been around my mom and her gymnastics team for a long time. And things might get tough after college. Life is going to throw us curveballs much worse than we ever saw at the plate. And you know what? It is always 20 on one with us Cass, we're not going anywhere."

That hit me like a ton of bricks. Although our proximity would change, regardless of distance, we would all have a home within each other. '20 on one' was real. It was not just something we said and not just something we committed to for one night. It was something we believed in, embraced, and held close to us. It wasn't something that would fade away after we won that final game.

Fast forward to November of 2012. It had been five months since our season ended and I had been living in Iowa working toward my master's degree at the University of Northern Iowa. I was a week away from my much-anticipated Thanksgiving break. It would be the first time I would be able to travel home to New York since the summer and the thought of seeing my family and friends was exciting. I got back in my car on Sunday morning after church and checked my phone. I had three missed calls from my mom and a voicemail from my dad. This was unusual. I called back right away and my dad answered the phone.

"What's going on?" I had this horrible feeling in my stomach and wished so badly for my dad to make me feel ridiculous for even worrying about anything in the first place.

"It's your grandma, Cass. She's not doing well."

"Do I need to come home?"

"Yes, you do."

A few days later I sat in my living room after an emotionally exhausting week. I was still in shock of my grandmother's passing. Anyone who knew our family knew how important my grandmother was and knew how difficult this would be for us all. I got up to check the mail and saw a small package with a return address of Tuscaloosa, Alabama. I opened the package to find twenty cards. Twenty sympathy cards addressed to my family and me. "It's always 20 on one, Cass. We're thinking about you." I couldn't believe it. I was so overwhelmed with how many of my former teammates, coaches, managers, trainers, and support staff not only contacted to me to express their condolences, but also checked up on me in the weeks and months following to see how I was doing. A few days later another package came from a teammate. This one addressed to not only my parents and me but to my grandfather as well. Then, flowers signed from the Alabama Softball family appeared on our doorstep.

Although there is nothing to make the loss of a loved one easier, there is always a way to provide comfort. At Alabama we talked about the difference between sympathy and empathy. Sympathy means that you feel bad for someone going through a difficult time. However empathy is putting yourself in that person's shoes and trying to understand what they are feeling and going through. My Alabama softball family showed my immediate family and me what the true meaning of empathy was. They cried with me, they felt the loss with me, and they provided a comfort I didn't think at the time was possible. When I got up in front of a packed church to speak for my grandmother, I knew they were all there with me, by my side. I didn't have to deal with this alone, and with 19 others by my side, I knew I could do it.

"We are going to warm up and stretch inside the locker room and then head over to one of the practice fields to hit." Coach Murphy explained.

This was good news so far, this made it sound like we'd be playing tonight. He continued, "The radar is showing a few hours where the rain should stop. We will try to get the game in then. First pitch should be around 10:00 pm."

'We're playing tonight!' That was the first thing that came to my mind. I felt like a kid again. The lights wouldn't go out just yet, our playtime would be extended for us just a little bit longer.

Despite having a smaller space than we were used to, we were able to complete our dynamic warm up inside the locker room. As always, once our warm up was complete Aly delivered her words of wisdom to us with the utmost passion. Aly left the circle and it came time for the team only huddle. We took one half step closer and linked our arms around each other uniting us as one. Another thought came to mind; I wondered how many more times I'd be able to be a part of a huddle. A teammate to my left and a teammate to my right, there was just something so special about it.

I smiled, looked down and began to clear my throat. I thought back to what I had written down in my journal earlier that day. What I had planned to share with my teammates in this huddle for the last time: 'Breathe. Relax. Have fun. Celebrate every little victory. Enjoy the final moments of this incredible ride. Know that we are an army of 20, banded together.' Just as I opened my mouth to speak...

"AH-CHOO."

"Bless you."

"Thank you."

I froze. These noises did not come from our huddle. Almost simultaneously as if it were planned, our team peered over to the origin of these sounds. We had completely forgotten the entire support staff was still in the locker room with us. These huddles were sacred and usually never heard by other people outside of the players on the team.

"Let's scoot that way." Amanda Locke pointed in the opposite direction of our newfound audience.

Instead of de-huddling, moving, and re-huddling we just shuffled our feet and slowly but surely found ourselves on the other side of the locker room. We were still well within earshot of everyone else. It must've been a comical scene to witness.

When it came time to hit, we were beyond thrilled to get out of the confines of the locker room. Everyone looked good hitting off Stephanie VanBrakle, our pitching coach. Her and Murphy would pitch batting practice to us before every game. Steph in particular, was a master at simulating the pitches we were likely to face come game time. Steph in her playing days was an All-American at the University of Alabama hailing from Chambersburg, Pennsylvania. I think there was a mutual agreement among our team that hitting off of Steph would be more difficult than any pitcher we would encounter at the plate.

A few of us were waiting in line for our turn to hit in the cage. As I was standing next to Jazlyn Lunceford she said, "So, we're gonna win tonight…right?" I started laughing. Jaz had been my roommate since our freshman year at Alabama. For four years we constantly left each other little notes and reminders around the apartment about some day winning a national championship. How it would feel, how we would celebrate, who would end up on the bottom of the dog pile; it wasn't just a goal, it was an obsession. For us, it was the epitome of ultimate success.

I can remember talking with her throughout our careers about just how difficult it would be to win it all. How much work would have to go into accomplishing this. How many sacrifices would have to be made. How many heartbreaks endured. This was not a dream for a normal human being. This was a goal that could lead you to experience the highest of highs but also the lowest of lows. Any time we were awake at 5:00am for conditioning we would look at each other and say something along the lines of, "We're gonna win it this year…right?"

I'm not sure why we always added the 'right?' at the end. Maybe it was to ensure that we stayed humble about this crazy dream of ours. We never wanted to feel like hoisting the trophy would be a definite. The "Right…?" served as a reminder that there was still work to be done in order for this dream to come true. Despite the question mark, we always said it with the conviction that someday it would be a reality.

"Yea. We are, Jaz." I finally replied. There wasn't a doubt in my mind, neither hers nor anyone else's. In order to pull this off, to reach the pinnacle of our sport, I firmly believed we had to be filled to the brim with confidence. There was no room for doubt at the top.

For three years prior we fought, we sacrificed, and gave everything we had to give. And for three years in a row we came up empty; no national championship ring, no celebration, we didn't even make it to the finals. Until this year. Our last year. After the loss the year before I received a text from Jaz stating, "I don't ever want to feel this way again." I couldn't agree more. We had knocked on the door so many times before, we were ready to finally bust through to the other side.

After we warmed up hitting we gathered our equipment and waited at the left field fence entrance to the stadium. I could hear the excitement from the fans in the stands. They too were aching for the game to begin. Younger fans were stretching over the railing, reaching for a chance at a high five from the players walking by. I'll have to admit, that was one of the coolest feelings. Playing at Alabama, and especially in the World Series, made you feel like a rock star.

After warming up our arms and taking a few ground balls, we waited along our dugout, eager to get going with the start of the game. We were ready. We had the right amount of excitement mixed with *energy and confidence. Reporter, Holly Rowe made a visit to talk to our team once again.*

"How do you think your team is going to handle this long rain delay and the potential for some bad weather later in the game?" She inquired.

"We're doing really well handling it right now. Holly, have you heard about our Oregon trip?" I replied.

Holly quickly flipped through her clipboard to find a blank page to write on. She got a pen ready in her hand, looked up at me and said, "No, I have not. Tell me."

CHAPTER 6

"LIFE IS NOT ABOUT WAITING FOR THE STORM TO PASS, IT'S ABOUT LEARNING TO DANCE IN THE RAIN."

I don't believe there is a better quote out there to perfectly exemplify handling adversity. Everyone is dealt a hand of cards in life. You can either complain about the misfortune of a bad hand or find a way to make the best of what you have. I know that every team in the country deals with hardship. I know there are some that deal with it better than others. I believe that the teams that can handle trials and tribulations most effectively are the ones that truly enjoy the journey that is the softball season. In the end, those are the teams that find themselves successful.

I enjoy telling stories about our team and experiences and most of them bring back great memories. However, it seems that whenever anyone mentions 'the Oregon trip,' our whole team winces. This trip was one for the books. It was riddled with struggles, each one teaching us countless lessons about the spirit of our team in 2012. We proved a lot to ourselves during that time and redefined what it meant to be resilient.

On Thursday, March 8, 2012 we left for our first southeastern conference game against the Kentucky Wildcats in Lexington, Kentucky. It would be a weeklong trip during our spring break that ended with Kayla Braud's home trip to Eugene, Oregon. We won our first SEC game the following night with extra inning heroics from Danae Hays and Courtney Conley. On Saturday the 10th we won our second game of the series in deciding fashion and enjoyed time to relax before our third and final game of the series on Sunday. That day was when the fun began.

Senior, Amanda Locke and sophomore, Ryan Iamurri walked downstairs to the hotel lobby and we could tell right away something was not right. They looked ill. Very, very ill. They had contracted an aggressive stomach virus that was clearly taking its toll on the both of them. Anyone who has played for a team is very aware of how sickness spreads like wild fire. We were athletes, we were all raised tough and most of the time, you would have to drag us off the field if we were ever hurt or sick. After seeing Amanda and Ryan barely able to sit up straight in the dugout we knew this was no ordinary virus. They both ended up sleeping on the bus as we completed our sweep of the Wildcats. It was a great win, the first three to start off the SEC season against a tough Kentucky opponent.

The post-game huddle was short and sweet as we were cutting it close for time for our flight to Oregon. We didn't even have the chance to shower afterwards. We grabbed our travel suits and changed on the bus as we raced to the airport. We made it in just enough time to get thirty-three people checked in and boarded on a flight. However, upon our arrival to the airport we were informed of a three-hour delay because of bad weather at our connection city of Houston, Texas.

We found ourselves in a predicament. Sweaty and smelly from our game, we sat and waited in the airport as all the shops and restaurants in the terminal closed down. I sat back and admired how our team found a way to make the best of our situation. Some tried to get ahead on school work while others played on their phones and chatted amongst themselves. Then the games began.

Whitney Larsen was a four-year starter at Alabama. She had graduated the year before and was named an All-American in her final year as she led the Tide to a third place finish at the Women's College World Series. Requiring one more year to finish her undergrad, Whitney committed to helping the team as a student assistant for the 2012 season. I think I can speak for the entire team when I say we were very happy to have her with us. Not only did Whitney bring a great perspective of both the game and our team to the table, she was also our source of comedic relief when we needed it the most. She was a major piece to the triumphs and victories we had that season.

As we began to get antsy in that airport, Whitney along with our trainer, Nick noticed that the designs on the airport floor looked like a court for the popular childhood game, 'Four Square.' However the tiling was more rectangular shaped so the rules had to be slightly adjusted. Normally this game is played with a larger ball, however at the time our team only possessed a small racquetball. As a select few began to play this game, a few others from the team began to get involved.

Let me try to explain something about our team: We were competitive beyond belief. We hated to lose more than anything and that feeling did not just apply to our ability to compete on the field. This was a feeling that carried over into every aspect of our lives. If there was something to be won, we would do everything in our power to make sure we were not on the losing end. The distraught feeling that came from a loss would far supersede the enjoyment of a victory. It was just how we were, how our brains were wired, and why we fit so well together at Bama. So, although this may have appeared as a fun-loving game amongst our team, this was actually a cutthroat battle. Nonetheless, for at least two hours the Alabama softball team competed with max-effort in a game of 'racquetball four-rectangle.'

Finally we were able to board our flight to Houston. In the cabin of this tiny plane were the thirty-three members of our team and staff, one other passenger, and a flight attendant. We still had not showered from our game and our ill teammates battling the stomach virus did not fare well with the turbulence on our flight. I felt bad for the one other passenger and flight attendant. Needless to say, we finally made it to Houston at midnight only to find out that our flight to Oregon had left with thirty-three empty seats.

If you have ever traveled through airports I'm sure you can understand how difficult it may be to schedule and reschedule travel plans. We had to find a way to get thirty-three people 2,300 miles before our game against the University of Oregon coming up in two days. Our director of operations, Kate Harris, handled this all like a champ. She has always been someone that decided the kind of day she would have when she woke up in the morning. She decided to be grateful and happy, and she made the decision to make it all about everyone else but herself. She is the ultimate definition of a selfless individual. Throughout all of the mayhem of a trip, Kate never once complained about our misfortune but instead put her head down, went to work, and got things done.

We patiently waited as our coaches and staff tried to figure out and plan the second half of our spring break trip. While waiting at the airport in Houston we scavenged for different ways to pass the time. We recruited a fellow traveler who happened to be a saxophonist and convinced him to play 'Sweet Home Alabama' at 1:30am in Houston's airport. I admired our ability to laugh, sing, and dance when it would have been very easy to be cranky, hungry, and tired.

We all had the opportunity to complain about our delays. Especially Kayla Braud. This was her homecoming. All of her family and friends were anxiously awaiting her Bama family to arrive in her hometown. If Kayla Braud wasn't pouting in the corner that meant none of us had the excuse to. The bottom line was that we were together and if we were together, we were going to find a way to enjoy it. As the clock wound down on my senior year as a member of this team, I found myself making more of an effort to cherish and appreciate my time with my teammates. It was very evident to all of us that we were a part of a special group.

After further miscommunication's we found ourselves at 2:30 am handing hotel vouchers that the airline provided us to a hotel that would not accept them. At this point, all we could do was laugh. Kate and the coaches came to the rescue once again and we were finally able to rest our heads on a pillow just a little past 4:00 am.

The next morning, just as Amanda and Ryan began to feel normal again from the sickness that sidelined them the day before, teammate Danae Hays and associate head coach, Alyson Habetz came down with the virus. They were out for the count and every movement for them took tremendous effort.

We waited around in our Houston hotel lobby for our 9:10 pm flight to Portland, Oregon. The next day we would be facing the fifth ranked team in the country, the University of Oregon. Most people would go crazy spending this much time with the same group of people for this long, but I think our team got closer as the trip continued. We watched spring training baseball and analyzed every one of the big-leaguers swings, discussing what we thought made them so successful.

We decided to get to the airport early for our late night flight and upon arrival discovered yet another error in our plans. Unbeknownst to us, half of our travel group was scheduled on the 9:10 pm flight while the other half of our team was scheduled to leave in thirty minutes. I wondered if fellow passengers appreciated our team's athleticism as we scrambled, jumped, and sprinted through security to get to our flight.

To make a long story short, both of our groups arrived safely in Portland by 1:00 am. We then had a two-hour drive to our hotel located in Eugene, Oregon. As we started our drive it began to snow, of course it did. Upon arriving at our hotel, two more members of our travel party sprinted to the bathroom. Whitney Larsen and manager, Chandler Whidden had contracted the bug. This virus did not look fun and we were doing everything in our power to avoid spreading it. If there was ever a world record for Purell use, we may have broken it that week. When our heads finally hit the pillow, it would be our second straight night falling asleep past 4:00 am.

The following day came quickly and it was obvious our team was exhausted. However, nobody dwelled on it or complained about it. By 10:00 am we arrived at a local elementary school to talk to kids about what it meant to be a student-athlete. Our energy and enthusiasm came straight from the excitement provided by the children that we had the opportunity to speak with. Once we left the school our focus shifted to the next task at hand. We had a game that night and we had a job to do: Win. One game, seven innings. We were determined to stay in the present and win one pitch at a time. We were focused on our goal and on what we could control in that moment. We kept our thoughts in check and made a conscious decision to not dwell on circumstances that were out of our control.

There are several strategies for dealing with adversity. Some allow difficult times to dictate their success. They allow the struggle to defeat them. These people throw in the towel and say, "This is too hard. Had I not been faced with adversity x, y, and z then I would have been successful." For those who have their focus locked in on a dream, quitting or giving up is never an acceptable option. When you hit a wall, you don't just find a way to get to the other side. Instead, you find a way to burst through the wall stronger with an even higher level of focus and intensity than before. It would have been very easy for our team to shrug our shoulders and say, "We aren't *supposed* to win this game against the number five ranked Oregon with only eight hours sleep over the course of two days. It's not *normal* to have energy to cheer and play with passion when we're this tired and fatigued. I *can't* give my best today."

It is so easy as an athlete to slip into this trap. It is natural to feel like our circumstances can dictate our thoughts, behaviors, attitude, and effort. We are human and these are very natural feelings. However, as a member of the Alabama Softball family, we made a promise to ourselves. We made a promise to be abnormal. To accomplish the things we weren't *supposed* to accomplish and to do things we didn't *feel* like doing. Why? Because champions do exactly that. It is abnormal to be a champion. Not everyone wins their last game of the season, not everyone hoists a trophy, and not everyone gets to dog pile after the last out. Only one team does, and they are not like the rest, they are champions. They do the things they don't feel like doing in order to become the best. When injury strikes, it is difficult and abnormal to relentlessly pursue ways to make yourself and your team better. When it is 6:00 am not every team *feels* like pushing their body to a new limit in the weight room but the teams that get to celebrate at the end of the season do it. They find a way, period.

Coach Alyson Habetz reminded us of this every single time we were exhausted and could barely breathe during conditioning, every time it was raining and below 40 degrees outside and it was time for practice. Anytime it got tough, we were reminded that out of the 289 softball teams in NCAA Division I there is only one champion left standing. There is only one team that gets to celebrate under the lights at Hall of Fame Stadium. There is only one team that gets to say, "We won it *all*." So in order to be that team, we knew we had to do things that all those other 288 teams didn't do. We had to be different.

When we took the field against Oregon that night, despite the illnesses, lack of sleep, as well as muscle soreness and fatigue, we gave everything we had in our tank. Maybe our tank was only half full, for others maybe it was at a quarter of a tank, but whatever we had, we made sure we were on empty by the time the game was done. In sports or in life, that is all that can really ever be asked of you; to give the best effort you possibly can in whatever you decide to do. *That* I believe is the true meaning of success. Are you willing to give everything you have so that you are left on empty by the time you are finished?

Winning that game against Oregon was not a coincidence. It was not a stroke of luck that we were able to pull the win off under our circumstances. It was because we had embraced our challenges prior to this point. When you are able to see failure and adversity as your friend, rather than a foe, you will put yourself in a position to burst through the wall triumphantly. Dealing with adversity successfully is not about standing there and taking punch after punch, it is about learning your opponent. It is about understanding where those punches came from, learning how to dodge the next one that may come, and then finally figuring out how to punch back. How to be fueled with fire and intensity after each defeat opposed to weak and disappointed.

Our team that season was training to win it all. We were training to fail successfully, to constantly fail forward. If the rain came, we made a decision to dance. We made a decision to embrace things that most would see as difficult barriers. For the 2012 season we did not lose to the same team twice the entire year. If a team ever beat us, the next game that followed was our best of the season. Whatever challenges came our way, we burned them away with this fire lit within all of us.

Ask yourself how comfortable you are when dealing with failure. As athletes on the field and in life we cannot always dictate our circumstances. We may strikeout, make an error, give up a walk off homerun, get injured, and have set backs that are out of our control. The ways in which you deal with what life throws your way will be how far you and your team will travel in your sport. Having a bad day is inevitable. However, that bad day does not define you as an athlete or a person. What is in your control is how much better you can make yourself on your worst days of the year. It is easy to give full effort and say you got better on an 'A' day. That 'A' day might have been when you aced a test, had a great batting practice, and family

members are in town to visit. That's when it's easy. How much
better would you get if you just found out you failed a test, got
yelled at by the coach for a terrible practice, and are homesick?
I challenge you to get better on *those* days. Understand and
embrace that finding success on those bad days will make
you so much better than you ever were on an 'A' day. Coach
Murphy would always tell us that we were a resilient group.
He cemented in our minds that as an Alabama Softball player
we would bend but we would never break. The next time you
are hit with adversity ask yourself what it will take to bend and
not break. Will you stay inside? Or dance in the rain?

"So because of all this, you feel like you guys are prepared for anything?"

I looked Holly Rowe right in her eyes and said, "Absolutely."

There was not a doubt in my mind and I felt so confident in answering her question. We were prepared for anything. Not because of everything we had already faced, but because we had learned the tools to overcome it all. We had shined in the face of adversity throughout the whole season and nothing this game threw at us could derail us from our goal. We were committed to giving the best effort we could possibly give in whatever we did tonight. We were a determined force, 20 strong.

Being that Oklahoma was the away team for the final game, the announcer began revealing their lineup first. We stood patiently in lines waiting in turn for our names to be echoed. It was obvious the majority of the crowd was in favor of Oklahoma. The World Series is hosted every year in Oklahoma City, just a short 30-minute drive from OU's campus. It was no surprise to us who the crowd was going to be cheering for.

I often hear of fans getting 'hooked' to a college or little league team. I've heard these teams get described as a 'breath of fresh air' compared to the professional teams. I tried to figure out why. Why so many people were drawn to these players at the lower levels. My answer can be encompassed in one word: Passion. There was no money at stake for any of us playing in this game. It was all about playing for the love of the sport. That is an attractive trait to have in a team. Most times you only see this type of passion in professional sports during playoffs. For this reason, a lot of fans only tune in for the final playoff games of each season. It's only when passion gets involved that athletes are elevated to this new height of competition. When the energy and emotion is tangible. When the atmosphere becomes so alive that the excitement emanates throughout the stadium with such ferocity that both athlete and spectator alike feel its force.

At the amateur level, this passion is the sole driving force. I've been to several professional games and have only felt the electricity from the fans on a few occasions. However, watching a team that plays with passion and excitement, I get that feeling from the crowd every time.

As Oklahoma's lineup was announced and the crowd cheered and clapped for each of their players, I took a brief moment to look at our team. We were calm, focused, confident, and in control. We were ready. There was not a single person in that dugout that wanted to be anywhere else but here. We were all in.

I looked at our uniforms. I was so happy we were wearing white. 'I always pictured us winning it all in white.' The thought quickly crept to my mind but just as quickly got pushed away by, 'Stay in the present.' There was no room to think about winning it all or celebrating now, we still had seven innings to play and the most important inning was the one coming up, the first.

Our cleats were all the same, black with a big crimson Nike swoosh outlined in white, stitched on both the inside and outside of our shoe. Our spikes were distressed from a season of wear and tear. The shine these cleats once had was long gone. The dirt and grass stains from every field in the SEC had been smeared on them. Our socks were also crimson with a white Nike swoosh on the front of our shins. Everyone on our team wore our socks high, a common theme amongst softball players. The socks were long enough so that there would be no skin showing and our pants could comfortably overlap at our knees. The pants were white, not too tight and not too loose. Each uniform custom fit for each player on our team. Along the outside of the pant leg ran a thin crimson piping from our waists to our knees.

The pants and the tops were connected by a thick leather belt. A belt that once showed a bright crimson was now worn and cracked. The belt no longer carried its original shape but instead was perfectly worn at the exact hole it needed to be buckled. Some of us didn't even have to look down anymore to fasten our belt; it instinctually fell right into place every time. It was a sign of the 67 games it had endured prior to this one. We all wore the same crimson dri-fit undershirt. On the right sleeve a Women's College World Series patch had been sewn on.

Some of us wore crimson sweatbands around our forearm. Some wore headbands. Chaunsey Bell had her now famous sparkle headband that spelled out 'Bama' positioned just to the right on top of her head. Jackey Branham donned her signature visor, a white one with a script crimson 'A.' Despite it being a night game, the members of the team who had been wearing eye black the entire season dared not to change anything now. We smeared the thick black paint under our eyes one final time. Applying eye black was an art and Lauren Sewell was known for her mastery of it. It took tremendous skill to achieve eye black with the perfect width, length, thickness, and symmetry.

Kayla Braud and Ryan Iamurri were the two on the team responsible for hairstyles. If anyone needed a braid on the team, they were the ones to ask. Especially with the rain that night, there were a lot of people on the team that requested a braid. A player's hairstyle can mean a lot to them. This may be one of those things that male athletes will just never understand. I can assure you that no female athlete wants to have a bad hair day while playing on national television. "If you look good, you play good…"

Finally, I looked at our uniform tops. They were white. I loved wearing white under the lights. They were a sleeveless style cut with buttons running down the middle. Crimson piping ran down and outlined the center of our uniform. A crimson Nike check was positioned on the front of our left shoulder. Eight inches below that was our number. Bold block numbers also colored crimson. On the back of our jersey carried our number, outlined and filled with the same crimson coloring. There were no last names on our jerseys and a part of me liked that. For that one night where we were fighting to win it all, no one needed to know who we were. They just needed to know who we played for: The Crimson Tide.

My favorite part of the jersey was positioned on the front along the right side. That is where the Alabama script "A" was located. There is something so special about looking down and seeing that "A" on your chest. I honestly can't describe it well enough. There have been many things in my life that I have been proud to be a part of. Each one I have given part of my identity to. When I was 11 I got to be a 'Huskie' and play on my first travel ball team. When I turned 15 I had the honor of being a 'Corn Husker' at my high school and later that year I was able to call myself a member of the 'Inferno.' These were all teams I was proud to make part of my identity. But there has been nothing that compares to wearing the "A." Nothing that compares to saying, 'I am a member of the Crimson Tide softball team. I am a student at the University of Alabama.' I will always be so honored to hand over a piece of my identity to that school and team. Every time I put my jersey on and got to button the uniform I would feel chills creep across my skin. It meant something to me and it was something special.

"Alright, you look good, Cass." Jennifer Fenton had just finished checking to see if my uniform was tucked in the 'right' way in the front and the back. I examined the front of her jersey, had her turn 180 degrees and examined the back. "Looks good Jen Fen." We perfected our tuck about 20 games into the season however made it a tradition to check each other's jerseys before every game just to be sure. 'That was the last time--' No. I quickly rushed that thought out of my mind. There was no room for any of that now. Now, it was game time.

"The University of Alabama!" Exclaimed the announcer. "With a record of 59 and 8 and making their 8th appearance at the WCWS..." I could feel the anticipation surging amongst us all. The announcer continued, "First the non-starters for the Alabama Crimson Tide..." Hall of Fame Stadium was ready for us. We were ready to be announced to the field. I could feel my heart rate elevate. One deep breath got me back to where I needed to be.

"#3 Keima Davis...#4 Jackey Branham...#6 Jordan Patterson...#11 Lauren Sewell...#17 Jadyn Spencer...#19 Danielle Richard...#21 Chaunsey Bell...#23 Leslie Jury...#24 Olivia Gibson and #32 Ryan Iamurri."

Our team aligned ourselves in two rows facing one another about five feet apart. Why do I know it was five feet a part? Because I always thought if we laid our 4'10" second baseman, Ryan down across the middle it would be about a perfect fit. No matter what you were feeling before any game, if there were nerves or doubts or insecurities, they'd all go away once we ran through that tunnel. It was as if going through that hallway lined with your family, lined with some of the best people in your life, reminded you of why you were here. It reminded you of how many people believed in you and how special this game was. Getting announced before the game was one of the best feelings I've ever experienced. It gets you fired up and calms you down all at the same time. Hearing our names boom across the loud speaker at any stadium was our reminder that we made it. We were all here for a reason, we had the talent, we had the passion, and we were all in this together.

One of my favorite things about my team was when we got announced before a game and had to run out to the baseline for the national anthem. Every one of us had a consistent appearance. Just by looking at us, there was no way to tell who was starting, who was sitting, who was slumping, or who was in the running for national player of the year. There was none of that. We were all members of the Crimson Tide. We all played a role, we all had a job to do, and we all were able to contribute. On June 6, 2012 at 9:50 pm, we ran through that tunnel ready to stand together and stand united. No player's role was bigger than another. If we were going to win this thing, we were going to need all twenty of us to get the job done.

CHAPTER 7

"FOR THE LOVE OF THE GAME."

They called themselves, "The Wolfpack." They were our non-starters, the players who were designated to the dugout for that particular game. We always said at Alabama that everyone has a specific job that they can do to make this team better. As an individual on a team, your job was to recognize your role, understand your role, and lastly execute your role to the best of your abilities.

When athletes are recruited to a top Division I program, they arrive on campus with the mentality that they will make their mark immediately. Their mind is set to make a difference on the field, contribute at the plate, and work to be the 'it' player they had always been in their athletic career. However, once these freshman show up at Alabama, they realize that everyone on the team is great. That everyone was the stud on their previous team. It becomes very obvious right away that over half of the members of this awesomely talented team are going to sit the bench during any given game. We understood on our team that it was not always the most talented nine players that played on the field. However, it was the nine players that played the best together and fit into the specific plan that needed to be executed to win that specific game.

Some years, no matter how hard a player worked, no matter how well they performed with the opportunities given to them, starting time was still not guaranteed. There may have been someone at 'their' position that was more suited to help the team. And that was the bottom line: How were we going to be most successful on the field together as a unit?

Upon arrival at the World Series in 2012, a reporter during a press conference asked Coach Murphy why he felt the team had done so well that year. He gave our non-starters an enormous amount of credit. He explained that the starters aren't the ones on the team that are usually unhappy. If there are ever any players on the team that are most likely to complain and cause a wrinkle, it's those that aren't getting as much playing time. Those are the players that can derail a team and cause a negative environment that no one wants to be around or be a part of.

However, not starting every game when that was all you were ever used to, is never an easy role to play. It is emotionally difficult to find yourself in this position. It is not a role for everyone. There were only a special few that could handle it the way our team did and they called themselves, "The Wolfpack." They had a special love for the game that is so rare to find.

Freshman catcher, Chaunsey Bell came to play at Alabama all the way from Indiana. She was a fierce competitor when she arrived on campus in the fall of 2011. I recently asked her about being a member of "The Wolfpack" and what it meant to her. She began talking immediately about how when she arrived her freshman year she was ready to make a statement. She wanted to make a difference the only way she knew how, by playing. However, she soon began to realize that starting every game wasn't going to be the role for her that year. Chaunsey instead explained to me her new role. She made it her job to push whoever was in front her every single day. She made it her responsibility to make the person starting in her intended position a better player, thus in return, the team would get better and the team would benefit.

"This was way bigger than everything. It was so much bigger than ourselves. There was such a special bond amongst us all." As Chaunsey explained this, I felt the goose bumps rise on the back of my neck.

On our team, no single person was above anyone else. The pitcher was not more important than any position player, a starter was not more important that a non-starter, and there was no one coach better than the others. We were a team and we were playing on the same level field. We were fighting for a chance to make an impact. We were fighting for a way to make a difference on our team any way we could. We knew if we were to ever receive championship rings, no ring would weigh heavier than the other. They would all be the same size.

The Wolfpack was established in the fall. There was a sense of pride amongst all of it's members which would change day to day depending on the lineup. They added a new position to the team, finding a way to impact the game without ever stepping foot on the playing field. They opened the team's eyes to how big of an influence those playing the dugout position could have on the outcome of a game.

Those who find themselves in the dugout possess a unique perspective and view. They can see extra hustle plays or observe a players swing that doesn't seem quite right. I always embraced an opportunity to receive feedback from a Wolfpack member. Their insight was never fogged with on-field chaos and confusion. They were focused and locked in on the game and were able to hone in on details that otherwise would have fallen through the cracks.

The Wolfpack found its natural leader in senior, Olivia Gibson. Upon arriving at Alabama in the fall of 2008 she found herself in a unique situation. She was battling for a position with someone in her own class. It is not often that two highly competitive players are recruited for the same position in a freshman class. Despite this unusual scenario, year in and year out Olivia found a way to contribute regardless of how much or how little playing time she had behind the plate. She trained every day in preparation for whatever her role may be. After all, the coaches would tell us all the time that no matter our job on the team, we never knew who would get the opportunity to play in the game. We had to be ready at all times.

There wasn't a blueprint of how to play the role of 'Wolfpack Leader' so Olivia had to figure it out on her own. She saw the necessity for a set of guidelines to be established for this position. It is incredibly difficult to sacrifice endless hours of work in the weight room and practice field and then come game time, not see your name written on the lineup card. It may sometimes feel that your efforts are not always being reciprocated. Olivia could have thrown her hands up, given up, said this was unfair, and not invested herself whole-heartedly into this team. That would have been the easy thing to do, the natural thing to do. However, despite how difficult of a role this was, Olivia took it on regardless of how enormous the task may have seemed. She willingly took the punches for us. Without her, the team would not have been successful. She took the pain and burden away from all of us and put it on herself. Olivia redistributed reliability and accountability to everyone on the team.

"Olivia was the one we could go to if we were ever struggling with our role or losing site about what was best for the team." Chaunsey explained.

"She never once made me feel guilty for feeling the way I did. Instead, she would provide the perfect level of comfort and support to make me feel better and get back on track."

Olivia became someone that other Wolfpack members could confide in about their emotional struggle with not playing as often as they were accustomed. She took on the responsibility of helping incoming freshman who were all-stars in their home state, understand their new job on the team. She was the quintessential model for how to take pride in the role you have been given. If you were a freshman not receiving as much playing time as you would like and you saw Olivia's smile in the dugout, there was no way you could throw a pity party for yourself.

It was imperative to the identity of the team that playing time did not dictate the attitude and effort put into practice. Everyone on our team took practice seriously. Practice was a time to push each other to the max. If you weren't starting as often, your job was to motivate whoever was starting at your position to be the best they are capable of being. If you were receiving a lot of opportunities to play, there would be nothing more disrespectful to the rest of your teammates than giving half effort at practice. Every member of our team had the mind set during practices and pre-game warm-ups that their number would be etched onto the lineup card. The Wolfpack took pride in bringing the fight and providing the intensity. Our dugout overflowed with fire and passion. It was something that was unmatched. Alabama Softball may have been national contenders in homeruns and stolen bases but there was no doubt about our dugout's energy. We led the country in that category.

Ask yourself, "How strong is your love for the game?" Is it strong enough to embrace your role regardless of your playing time? Ask yourself if you would rather win a national championship or be an All-American. Picture this scenario: If you were asked to invest your life savings into something, would you do it? What if best case scenario entitled you to 40-50% of your investment back. In reality, the experts predict that you'll only see about a 20-30% return on your savings. Would you invest? Hopefully your answer is no. However, this is softball. That is our sport. We are constantly failing at the plate. In hitting, we fail frequently and rarely ever does a player succeed more than they fail. Most players at their best will hit .350 at an elite level. The majority will bat .200-.250 and some of us don't even get the opportunity to have an at-bat at all. How strong is your love? Would you condition all fall and winter, hit every day to work on your swing, do all your required lifting and more on top of that to have a chance of failing over and over again at the plate?

In order to play softball you can't just like it. You *have* to love it. You have to have a love so strong that you'd be willing to sacrifice it all. You must be so head over heels in love with this game and your team that you could go into the worst slump of your life and still come back for more. That you could lose on a walk-off homerun to end your season and your love is still unwavering.

I've had younger players getting recruited ask me my opinion on where they should consider playing in college. Option A would allow them to probably start all four years. With the level of competition in that particular conference, they would have a good chance of being named to the All-Conference team too. Option B is different. Option B competes in a dominant conference. There is no guarantee with the caliber of athletes being recruited to that program that they will have playing time. They would have to be at their best in order to contribute on the playing field at this option B. Although there is a long list of criteria to consider when selecting a college, the first question I ask these athletes is, "How much do you love the game?" If you didn't start would you still love the game? If you had to wake up every morning and train until you could barely walk would you still love the game? If the answer is 'yes,' then I challenge you to work for option B. There is no greater fulfillment than becoming the best you can possibly be at the one thing you love. The one thing you have a burning desire and passion for. If the answer is 'yes' then understand you are in for an uphill battle. That loving the game is a burden given to the few who can truly handle the responsibilities for a love this strong. Know that there are few people in this country capable of loving something after experiencing the pain this sport can cause. If your answer is 'yes,' then buckle up and enjoy the ride. Because you are about to go on a rollercoaster ride that will take you to the highest of highs but potentially the lowest of lows.

Anytime there may be a low point in the season, our coaches seemed to know exactly what to do to remind us of our love for the game. Before one practice we were shown a ten minute video called, 'The Little Team.' It was about a young soccer team that was having a bit of a difficult season. They had been losing a lot, every game to be exact. Not only had they lost every game of their season, they had not scored a single goal. To make matters worse, they had allowed 271. However, when observing the interviews with these young players, there was no frustration or defeat about them. They instead showed a love for a game only a child could have.

"We'll score goals when we grow old." States one of the children. When asked what he would do if he himself scored a goal one day, he could hardly sit still. His eyes changed to a more slanted shape as his cheeks stretched from his smile. He rocked back and forth and excitedly exclaimed, "And if one day I score, I'd be so happy that I'll fly!" How could we not all smile and recheck our situation. Here we were with an opportunity to play for one of the best softball teams in the nation. There was no way we could complain about a slump or feel stressed about managing schoolwork and being an athlete. Instead we had a newfound appreciation for the game we love.

There were members of our Wolfpack that were promised more playing time and more scholarship money somewhere else, but they chose Alabama. They knew coming to Alabama would not only make them the best softball player they could be, but they would reach the pinnacle of a bond unknown to many. This bond experienced amongst the Alabama Softball family would help make them the best possible version of themselves by the time they graduated.

In order to play this role, as a member of the Wolfpack, you couldn't have any ordinary love for your sport. Not even close. You must have a genuine care for the people you play with in order for this to work. This is a role only for the rare hearted. Only for the outliers and those that can fight what feels 'natural.' What is unnatural is to lose yourself in a celebration when your teammate makes a diving catch. What is unnatural is to be so invested in the success of your team that you are willing to sacrifice what is best for you for what is best for the rest. What is unnatural is to have a 'we before me' attitude in every decision you make on and off the field. Our Wolfpack did that for us, for the team. They were the driving force the entire season behind the beat of our heart. They provided the rhythm, kept the blood flowing, and assured a steady beat was maintained. On June 6, 2012 when I felt all of our hearts beating together as one, I knew exactly the reason why: Every member had a love for the game and a love for this team.

"The starting lineup for the Crimson Tide, leading off in left field, #1, Kayla Braud!"

I heard the loyal Bama fans behind the third base dugout erupt once again. How extraordinarily special it was to have a fan base like we did. Each one of us were fortunate enough to have family members in the crowd. So many people in our lives that were willing to sacrifice their time to share in a once in a lifetime moment with us.

"Starting in centerfield batting second, #7, Jennifer Fenton." The announcer continued on.

Beyond our family and friends was our extended family, the Alabama softball fans. They were one of a kind. They were impressively knowledgeable about the game, were willing to go to battle to defend every single one of us and best of all, they absolutely hated losing more than anything in this world. They had supported us through thick and thin, rain or shine. Our stadium, The Rhoads House, would be packed with 2,000 plus during mid-week non-conference games. If we ever had an SEC rival come to town, the stadium held over 4,500 people, all cheering for us. How many people in this world get to have a fan base when they're 18 and right out of high school? How many college students get to sign autographs? Or have people tweet and Facebook message them saying, "You are my role model!" or "I am your biggest fan!" How unique is it to have people recognize you at a restaurant and request to have their picture taken with you? You really do get a small taste of stardom as a student athlete. Our fans were an awesome support group while we were all away from home and just another reminder that we were playing this game for something bigger than ourselves.

"Batting third and playing shortstop, #10 Kaila Hunt."

The leader of the Crimson Tide fan base was none other than Mrs. Emily Pitek Clifford. She is a well-known icon at Alabama softball games for being the most enthusiastic and passionate fan. She is actually an inaugural member of the 'ESPN Hall of Fans' and is known for her crimson striped overalls and iconic pink sombrero that she wore to every game. Beyond her outfit and hilarious cheers, what goes unnoticed is how much she impacted any game she was there for. She was our edge. Anyone who says that the crowd doesn't play a role in a game has never felt it's force. That's what home field advantage is. It's that feeling again. The one you can't measure or evaluate, you can only sense its distinct impact.

"Batting fourth for the Tide and pitching in the circle, #33 Jackie Traina."

It's that feeling you get when you yell to cheer for a teammate but you can't hear yourself. You can't even feel the vibrations from your vocal chords because the noise from the crowd is so deafening. The feeling that escalates and sends off alarms in your mind that tells you, 'This is something big.' Momentum is a category that doesn't show up in any statistics book. However, if you listen to announcers during any game, they talk about it a lot. "'The momentum has shifted.' 'They are gaining momentum now!', 'Momentum is on their side.'" Without passion, momentum does not exist. Passion is a flame that burns within a team. There are so many variables that can add to it, and yet so many that can let it die out. The energy that the fans created shifted that momentum to our side. It is what fueled our passion. Emily was our match. She ignited the crowd, she ignited the passion and she caused momentum to constantly fall in our favor. She was a game changer for the Alabama softball team.

"Batting fifth for the Tide, the first baseman, #18, Cassie Reilly-Boccia."

I took a deep breath, looked down the tunnel of my teammates and ran through high fiving each of the remaining players who had not yet been announced. At the end, as always was Alyson Habetz. Every human is capable of smiling but Aly's told a story. She had elation on her face. She had a genuine smile that said what words fell short on explaining. High fiving her before running out onto the field for the last time was extremely special for me, as I'm sure it was for every Tide player that came before me and will come after me.

With my glove tucked under my right arm, I sprinted onto the field toward my position at first and heard the noise my metal cleats made as they scratched the dirt below.

"Let's go to work today, Jack!" I told her as I ran by Jackie who was standing in the pitching circle. I could not stop smiling. I couldn't help it. I was about to play softball! The one thing I loved the most and how lucky am I to do it with the people I cherished by my side? I was blessed beyond belief. I couldn't help but be so thankful for where I was in that present moment. How many athletes knew when their last game would be? How many get to play knowing they have an opportunity to win it all?

"Batting sixth and catching for the Tide, #12, Kendall Dawson."

Kendall came through the tunnel of the only three remaining players. At the end of the line, Aly handed Kendall her crimson Easton catching helmet. She then found her place behind home plate with all of her gear on and looking like a force to be reckoned with.

"Batting seventh, the designated player, #22, Amanda Locke."

Being at first base, I was in very close proximity to the opposing team who was standing along the first base line. I didn't feel them though, all I could focus on was my teammates. During that time, there was no room in my heart for anything else other than my team. My heart was full with them, there was no hate or ill feelings towards the opposition, there was just a competitive drive to achieve something with my team that had never been done before.

"Batting eighth and playing third base, #9, Courtney Conley."

Today was teammate Jackey Branham's 21ˢᵗ birthday. The entire season we had talked about winning a national championship on the day she turned 21. It was surreal that the day was finally here. I saw her mom in the stands proudly holding a 'Happy 21ˢᵗ Jackey!' sign in the crowd. We were all so excited and overjoyed to be playing on that field, I'm pretty sure we all felt like it was our birthday too.

"Batting ninth and playing right field, #2, Jazlyn Lunceford."

For a split second I let my mind travel to the future. This would be the last time I took the field with my class. For Jazlyn Lunceford, Jennifer Fenton, Olivia Gibson, Amanda Locke, Kendall Dawson, and I, this was our last time. Last time on this field, last time in this jersey, last time together.

'Stay in the present!' I snapped out of the thought just as quickly as it came to me.

"Playing second base, the designated player, #15, Danae Hays."

We were ready. We were all so ready. Our show was about to start. We were about to begin this game that we had been waiting three hours for, been waiting all day for, been waiting our entire careers for.

"Ladies and gentlemen we ask that you remove your caps and please rise for the playing of our national anthem."

I watched as each one of my teammates placed our gloves on the ground to the left of us. We stood facing the American flag positioned in centerfield with our heels only a few inches apart and our toes pointed slightly out. One by one we moved our left hand behind our backs and rested our tightened fist just above our belts. Next, our right hand found it's home across our heart. We were still, like statues. The music began to play. Instantly my body was immersed in chills. There was something special about the anthem. A reminder of something so much bigger than ourselves.

It was the calm before the storm. When the anthem began, you knew game time was only moments away. As the song continued on, I stared at the flag and I thought of what was written on my wrist. Something I wrote on my wrist before every game I ever played in an Alabama uniform. Although it was smeared and barely legible now, I knew it was there and I knew exactly what it said. It read, "Your Best." It was my reminder that I could do no more and I would never give any less. It was comforting and without fail no matter the butterflies that began to flutter in my stomach, thinking of those words on my wrist brought me back to where I needed to be.

Not a single one of us moved until three seconds after the final note of the anthem echoed across Hall of Fame stadium. We then simultaneously bent over, picked up our gloves and turned over our right shoulder to face the field.

"Woooo! Happy Game-Day, Jack! Let's go to work today!" The smile was still cemented on my face. There was no fear, no doubt, no insecurities. We were in the cage with failure now and we were staring it square in the face. With 20 voices strong we said, "We are not afraid of you."

Chapter 8

"Confidence must blind 'logic'"

Your confidence must be so rock solid that it blinds 'logic.' I put 'logic' in quotes because what really is logic? 'Logic' is what makes sense on paper. It says that the top seed should always beat the underdog. 'Logic' is made up of rankings, statistics, and cold-hard facts. But if 'logic' and what is on paper really mattered that much, then why would anyone ever play the game? Why not decide games before they're played based on stats, reporters opinions, and 'logic.' It's because the *game* doesn't know who it 'supposed' to win. The game doesn't know who has the nicer uniforms, or the better record, or the most talented players. All the game knows is that it's not always the best team that wins, it's the team that plays the best on the day of the game that wins.

At the WCWS in 2012 when we beat the number one seed in the semi-final round we were extremely excited. But we were not shocked. We played the entire World Series with a supreme confidence like nothing I have ever experienced. We knew the entire year, every time we gave full effort during a conditioning session, every time we lifted more weight than we thought we could, or got better at practice on a 'B' day, we were making payments. We were making payments for a trophy we were planning to pick up in June. When we showed up in Oklahoma City after ten months of training, conditioning, practicing, and playing, there was not a doubt in our mind what we were there to do. We were there to pick up what was rightfully ours. Why was it rightfully ours? Because we paid for it. We made payment after payment and we knew that it was all paid off. All we were there to do is take something that was always ours to begin with.

This mentality takes time. Just like a muscle, it must be something you train for and work at to make better. We worked to have confidence in everything we did, even when we didn't feel that great. Think about our game. If you are hitting .350, which is an excellent batting average, you are failing 65% of the time. I can't think of another sport or profession where the definition of success comes with so much failure. The sport of softball becomes not just about finding ways to be successful, but instead finding ways to deal with failure. Finding ways to let it go and focus on the most important pitch, the next one that's about to come. When you strike out or make an error, it is going to be human nature to not feel great about yourself. It's *easy* to feel sorry for yourself, it's *easy* to check out and say, "I'm not good enough." It takes a talented and mentally skilled individual to still have confidence after failure. It all starts with the way you act. Your body language can dictate so much about you and your game. There may be times where you have to remind yourself to straighten your posture, put your shoulders back, and your chin up. It will be human nature to do the exact opposite. Our strength and conditioning coach, Michelle Diltz would constantly remind us to have great posture. She didn't just say this to help with our physical strength, she also did this to improve our mental strength.

We made the effort to practice the tough situations. Failing is always an opportunity to improve yourself. Two hundreds pounds is a lot of weight that if mishandled could cause a lot of damage. However, 200lbs could also, with focus, precision, and technique be squatted, thus making you stronger. That is what failure is. It is a weight that can cause damage or make you better. You are the only one who decides what to do with it. Former Yankee great, Yogi Berra is the author to some of the greatest quotes known to baseball. My favorite one is, "Baseball is 90% mental, the other half physical." Anyone with a basic understanding of math can see the humor in this statement. I often ask players I work with, "If the game truly is 90% mental, why don't we practice ground balls and hitting for ten minutes and spend the rest of practice sitting down working on the mental game?" They usually smirk at the ridiculousness of this question.

The mental game must be practiced simultaneously with the physical game. You should rejoice in making an error in practice because you will now have an opportunity to practice how you would handle a situation like this in a game. Here is the bottom line: You are going to fail and things will not always go your way. Everyone will experience the weight of failure. The only question left to answer is, are you going to train so the weight eventually feels lighter? Or will you let it pile up until you are buried?

We were always searching for ways to boost our confidence, always trying to find ways to help get mentally stronger from the weight. At the beginning of the season we drew a house on our dry-erase board. We were given an activity to build a strong foundation for the house that was the Alabama Softball team. A house with a poor foundation crumbles, but a house built on a strong foundation can weather any storm sent its way. We took post-it notes and began writing down reasons why we should be confident, why our team this year was going to endure failures that were inevitably headed our way. One by one we placed the post-it notes under our house as if we were laying bricks: "Our team speed is something no one can practice for."; "We have a pitching staff that has each other's backs."; "Our senior class has been through it all and is willing to lead us from the front."; "Our coaching staff is the best in the country and is constantly finding new ways to better themselves and us."; "We have a *presence* at the plate, we strut to our at-bat, we do not walk."; "Everyone on our team takes advantage of opportunities."; "We are SELFLESS."; "We are able to recognize and celebrate the little things." The reasons for our team to be confident seemed endless.

Once the final two teams were locked in to the championship series in OKC, it was clear Alabama wasn't the favorite to win it all. We didn't have to watch T.V. or read social media to figure it out. Everyone said that Oklahoma's pitcher, the National Player of the Year, was *unstoppable*. She was the *best pitcher in the country*, and that the Alabama hitters were not equipped to handle her. 'Logic' is like a poison. It can seep into your ear, travel to your brain and start rewiring your thoughts. 'Logic' has the power to make your palms sweat, your knees shake, and your stomach churn. However, there is an antidote. It's confidence.

Confidence is not a light switch. It's not something that you can turn on and off. Confidence is something you as an athlete and you as a *team* train for. You must practice having confidence at all times. Confidence at the beginning of the season starts out jogging. As it's running it gets shot at, spit on, and tripped. It's going to fall down. It's going to want to quit. But eventually, every time you as a team act confidently even when you don't feel like it, confidence gets back up from its knees. Anytime you as a team accomplish a goal that others thought was not possible... confidence begins running. Any time you as a team come together and achieve something that none of you as an individual would have ever been able to accomplish on your own, confidence starts sprinting. By the time you get to playoffs, where it really matters, confidence is in a full sprint, down hill at 100 mph and it's not stopping.

At the peak of confidence, it doesn't matter what the reporters say. It doesn't matter if the team you have to beat twice beats you the first game and sticks your backs up against the wall. None of that matters because your confidence has been battle tested. It is a warrior that is bruised, battered, and scraped. After we lost the first game to Oklahoma, we came back and scored eight runs off of them in the second game. They had to take out their National Player of the Year pitcher. The one who was 'unstoppable.' There was absolutely *nothing* you could have told us that could've convinced us they were the better team. When we came back for game three to decide the national champion, we were still sure. There was no doubt. Not during the three-hour rain delay, not after their pitcher retired our first nine batters in a row. Not after their team took a 3-0 lead into the fourth inning. Our confidence was too strong; it had been through too much, it could not be shook. It could not be derailed. If we were to win the national championship, we would be excited, but we would not be shocked. We would finally be taking home what we had paid for, we would be taking home *our* trophy.

"Rollll Tiiiide! Roollll Tiiiide!" Alabama's fans were chanting over the third base dugout.

"OU! OU!" Oklahoma's fans would respond.

Jackie threw her fifth and final warm-up pitch. Kendall's mitt popped and just as quickly as it entered her glove, our All-SEC defensive catcher removed the ball from her mitt, twisted her shoulders and torso as she firmly planted her front foot and fired a missile to second base all in one swift motion.

"Nice throw!" Kaila Hunt responded from second base.

Warm-ups were over. It was time for the first pitch. You could feel the excitement and energy in the air. Jackie got the ball in the circle. She turned around to face the batter, planted her left foot on the rubber followed by her right. She stared at Kendall's signs waiting to see what pitch she'd throw first as she lightly blew on the fingers of her bare hand.

"Rollll Tide! Rollll Tide!", "OU! OU!" The crowds chanting was endless.

The on-field chatter continued as well. *"Nobody better, Jack!", "Here we go! Ball on the ground we're headed one, outties shoot two!"*

There was so much noise on the field if you tried to listen for it. Most of the time as an athlete we are too focused to hear anything from the stands. We were trained to zone out anything above and beyond the threshold of the dugout. As a first baseman, I made it my personal responsibility to be the noise barrier between our pitcher and the other team's dugout. I would talk to my pitcher until my mouth was dry. Maybe sometimes my pitcher found it useful, maybe other times she was too zoned in to hear anything at all. Regardless, I wanted her ear trained to my voice. If she needed a familiar voice to listen to, I wanted it to be her teammate and not the talk from the opposing team's dugout or stands.

"Alright, here we go Jack, nobody better than you, let's win this pitch right here."

I tried to help keep my pitcher motivated and focused in the present. I knew the most important pitch in any at-bat would be the next one. As a team, we had a goal of winning one pitch at a time, if we did that we were going to put ourselves in a good position to be successful in the end.

The top of the first flew by quickly. One, two, three. Jackie shut the door on their hitters and it was our turn to bat. Once the third out was recorded our team sprinted off the field, we were eager to get a bat in our hands. Off the field we huddled in front of the third base dugout, "Yeah Tide!" "Here we go Bama!" I wish so badly more people could feel the excitement that was condensed in that one huddle.

All of our hands came toward the middle, Aly held them tight on the top and bottom, "Attack right here, Bama!" she said. The team replied with, "Attack hard, score first, no mercy Bama!" The last note of 'Bama' echoed in our huddle. It was something we said before our first at-bats every single game. Once the last note was said, we dispersed. The Wolfpack took off down the third base line to stay loose, Kayla Braud and Jennifer Fenton popped out of the dugout with their helmets, batting gloves, and bats ready to go to battle for us. The third batter due up that inning got her equipment ready and promptly took her spot on the first step of the dugout reviewing her hitting charts from the previous two games. The fourth batter due up gathered her gear, sat on the bench with her head down and did some last minute visualizations.

"She's been trying to come in on you all series. I'd stick with the game plan, crowd the plate and look to crush that curve ball." Whitney Larsen was talking with Kaila Hunt about the plan of attack as they reviewed the hitting charts.

"You guys set the tone for us. When you get on, we score. You guys are seeing the ball huge right now." Ryan Iamurri was leaning *over the dugout with her hand over her mouth talking to our number one and two batters due up.*

"Yeah, Bama!" Nick Seiler paced the dugout spreading his excitement to everyone he passed.

"We ready to roll?" Amanda Locke asked as she looked around the dugout. After getting a reassuring nod from those in the general vicinity, she began the pregame tradition.

"RO-OLL!" Amanda yelled out.

"RO-OLL!" The team responded.

"Now coming to the plate for the Alabama Crimson Tide, number 1, Kayla Braud." The announcer boomed.

"RO-OOLLLL!"

"RO-OOLLLL!"

After every form of the word 'roll' was yelled from Amanda, came the same reply from the dugout. Kayla did her routine and sifted her feet through the dirt up and down the batter's box. She was ridding that box of any previous footprints. For this at-bat, this would be her box and no one else's. She placed one foot in the batter's box, raised her left hand to the umpire and looked up at Murphy in the third base coaches box with an intensity in her eyes that I have never seen worn on any other human being.

"ROLL!"

"ROLL!"

The dugout was getting loud. The anticipation could be felt from the Bama faithful above our dugout. Finally, Kayla planted her front foot, took her left hand, and placed it on the bat, she was ready. Ready for whatever was to come her way.

I could feel my heart begin to pound.

"Rollll..." Amanda's voice and the team's voice became one as we awaited the first pitch from their team. On release of the pitch on queue, our team replied with a "Tide! Roll!" completing the cheer.

"Strike!" yelled the umpire. And we were off.

CHAPTER 9

"BE JUST AS HAPPY FOR YOUR TEAMMATES SUCCESS AS IF IT WERE YOUR OWN."

I t was always about the team. No matter what. I asked a recruit one time why they were attracted to the Alabama Softball program. She replied with, "I really like how there has never been a player bigger than the program. Alabama Softball as a whole has always been the most important thing." I loved that answer, because it held so much truth. Our program thrived when every player was more concerned about their teammates' success than they were their own.

The title of this chapter was a fundamental building block of the Alabama Softball program. Since day one, this was engrained into our mindset as players. This was not something that could be faked, nor was this a skill that could be practiced. Could you sit on the bench while your teammate shined on the field and celebrate her success without any reservations? Without any sign of hesitation?

This might be tough for some people but this was *exactly* what would allow us to compete for the biggest prize in college softball. Our team was composed of selfless players that showed genuine support for one another. Of course everyone wanted to play every game. We were competitive and we loved the game of softball. To each individual on the team, softball was the thing that we did best. In reality not everyone had an opportunity to play. Our game, this game of softball, does not owe us anything in return for our hard work. Just because we gave our best effort in practice did not guarantee a 4-4 game every time we competed. Even if we took the most ground balls out of any defense in the country, it did not guarantee an errorless season. That's what makes this game so special. It is what makes the people who play it so extraordinary.

Someone will never be able to play for a true team if they are constantly rejoicing in their own achievements. Instead, members of a true team must radiate with pure joy for the victories of their teammates. This is when a player will find themselves lost in celebrating another's triumphs without hesitation. If you find yourself exuding more passion for your own success than you do your teammates success, you're missing out on one of the most special parts of this game.

In 2009, during my freshman year, Alabama was playing in the Women's College World Series in an elimination game against the Arizona State Sun Devils. Just the year before the Sun Devils were national champions and had ended Alabama's season during their quest for the championship trophy. It was a Saturday night, the winner would advance to the semi-finals on Sunday and the loser would go home. We were losing 2-0 in the bottom of the fourth inning and had the bases loaded with two outs and our four-time All-American senior leader,

Brittany Rogers coming to the plate. As the game was winding down, this could potentially be Brittany's last at-bat of her playing career.

Brittany was by nature a lefty slap hitter. For those unfamiliar with softball this was a type of hit that was concentrated on precision and touch, opposed to power and force. Brittany's game was geared toward placing the ball for base hits, not crushing the ball over the fence. Coach Murphy walked down the third baseline as Brittany approached home plate for her at bat and stuck his head in the dugout.

"Jaz. Get ready. You're hitting." He said.

Freshman, Jazlyn Lunceford would pinch hit for senior, Brittany Rogers. As always our team trusted Coach Murphy's decision making. Jaz had great batting practice sessions the whole week and would be able to potentially get an extra base hit to score more runs with the bases loaded opposed to a well placed single from Brittany. Our team never second-guessed the decision. What we didn't know at the time was that the ESPN announcers, those watching at home, and just about everyone in the stands had different thoughts crossing their mind.

"Taking out your senior leader for a freshman? I don't know. I think you gotta go with what got you here. Brittany Rogers was a big reason they got here last year and a big reason they got here this year," ESPN announcer John Kruk stated. In the background of the doubt coming from the analysis booth, Brittany Rogers' voice pierced through the microphones, "Fight for us, Jaz! Fight for us! We believe it!"

Put yourself in Brittany's shoes for a minute. You are a four time All-American, All-SEC, All-everything. You have given yourself completely for your team and have done so much for this program on and off the field. You are walking up to the plate with an opportunity to change the game with the bases loaded. This could very well be the final at-bat of your career and Murphy calls your name back to put in a freshman instead. A freshman who had not played in a game in over three weeks. A freshman who had not had a hit in over a month. A freshman who had never played in a playoff game before, let alone had an at-bat at the Women's College World Series. How would you react?

Brittany calmly hung her bat up, removed her helmet from the top of her head, and placed it in the cubby. She took off her batting gloves and gently set them down as well. She then got to the top step of the dugout and yelled. She yelled for her teammate, for her sister. She gave everything she had so that Jaz knew she wasn't alone at the plate. When you play at the World Series there are cameras and microphones everywhere and they were all on Brittany. I think they were waiting to see her slip up. To catch her making a comment about how she wasn't batting or to throw her bat or slam her helmet down in frustration. She did none of these things. That was not the senior leader she was. She cared about the success of her team more than she did her own personal success. Those All-American trophies? They came as a by-product of Brittany giving everything she had for her team to win it all. If she had ran out onto the field every game with an All-American trophy in mind instead of a National Championship trophy, I honestly don't think she would have won all those personal accolades along the way.

Now, back to Jaz. When you ride a rollercoaster, at a certain point you may feel the distinct sensation of allowing yourself to get scared. As your cart ascends to the highest peak of the ride, the worst thing you can possibly do is look down. Fixing your eyes on the track in front of you is the only way to remain calm. The second you glance over the edge of your cart to see the ground below, your anxieties kick in. Your heart begins to race, your palms begin to sweat, your breathing becomes rushed and shallow and your thoughts become clouded. The only way to keep your cool is to ignore the height you've climbed. Letting yourself acknowledge the potential to fall will lead your mind to spin into a of whirlwind of panicked "what ifs." It is imperative to keep your focus on that track ahead. As I watched Jaz step up to the plate in that moment, I knew that she had locked in on the track. At the very pinnacle of this ride, there was no way she was going to look down.

Her ride started when Murphy poked his head in the dugout and told her to get ready. She put her batting gloves on, placed her white helmet with the crimson script "A" on her head, and picked out her bat; her weapon of choice. Elevating to a new level, Jaz walked up the steps that led from the dugout to the field. Click, click, her cart began to climb.

"Now batting for the Crimson Tide, #2, Jazlyn Lunceford." The announcers voice echoed into Hall of Fame Stadium.

Click, Click, still rising.

The excited murmur of 8,475 fans was now locked in on her and her at bat.

Click, click.

I could tell by Jaz's body language she hadn't looked down yet. She was still calm and in control. First pitch of the at-bat, Jaz took it for ball one.

"You can do this, Jaz! Fight for it, Jaz!" Brittany yelled from the dugout. On the second pitch, Jaz's bat flew through the strike zone and foul tipped a ball for her first strike.

"Woo! Jaz you take your hacks up there!" another teammate yelled from the dugout.

"Hey! That swing looked good, Jaz!" I yelled in hopes of Jaz hearing me, but it was clear that no outside noise was going to reach her.

Click, click, the cart kept rising higher and higher with each and every pitch. Pitch number three was a ball high and outside.

"Great job, Jaz! Great job!" Brittany was at the plate with her on every pitch. Pitch number four was fouled off to the left side and into the stands. The count was now 2-2. Two strikes, two outs, bases loaded, down by two.

Click.

Click.

"Stay in there, Jaz, you can do this!" Jaz's focus was straight ahead. She never once looked down. Pitch five, another foul.

Click.

"Fight for us! Fight! Fight!" Brittany's voice was now hoarse. These were not hollow cheers for the cameras. They were heavily weighted with intensity and passion. Brittany wanted this so badly for Jaz and for the team.

"Let's go Jaz-lyn! Let's go Jaz-lyn!" The crowd chanted away.

Click, click. click.

The cart continued to ascend. Just the slightest glance down could cause a derailment.

Jaz put one foot in the batter's box. She stared in the direction of the pitcher and took one deep breath. She lightly swayed her bat back and forth. Her face was calm, but her stance held a confident rhythm; she had the perfect balance of intensity and focus.

The Arizona State pitcher delivered the sixth and final pitch of the at-bat to Jaz.

'Pop!' The ball soared off Jaz's bat. Brittany screamed. She was the first one I heard. Then I heard the roar. I felt the crowd. My stomach dropped.

I didn't need to watch the ball clear the fence. I didn't need to see it. I already knew. I could feel it. Hall of Fame Stadium shook. The atmosphere had become electrified. Jazlyn Lunceford had just hit a grand slam over the left field fence. There was a mad dash for home plate to maul Jaz. And the first person there? Brittany. She was jumping up and down screaming her lungs out. She was just as happy for Jaz's success as if it were her own. We all were.

"A pinch hit grand slam puts Alabama up 4–2 and Patrick Murphy looks like a genius!" the ESPN announcer exclaimed. Jaz could finally look down and enjoy the ride. Rounding the bases and getting greeted at home plate by a wave of crimson and white jerseys. I wonder if there is a better feeling than that. I don't think you could find teammates happier anywhere else. We were elated to celebrate in Jaz's success with her.

One week earlier we had been back in Tuscaloosa on our home field preparing for the World Series in our final practice of the season. Having never experienced the WCWS myself, I looked at Brittany Rogers and asked, "What is one word to describe the World Series, Britt?" A big smile came across her face and she said, "It's electric, Cass. It's something you can really feel."

That night when Jaz made contact with the ball I finally knew what Britt meant.

Sharing in a teammate's accomplishments can be one of the most rewarding feelings. As if being successful on the field isn't exciting enough, imagine seeing your teammates jumping out of the dugout with so much joy and passion pouring into you.

It is an energy that feeds off of one another and multiplies with ferocity. It gains such momentum that it cannot be trumped and it cannot be extinguished.

There's only one thing that could have taken away from Jaz's amazing feat. One thing that could have dulled the excitement of such an incredible moment. Something that could have taken away the excitement of Jaz's ESPN interview, the sixty-five text messages waiting on her phone from friends and family congratulating and celebrating with her, or the hundreds of fans who waited to get her autograph after the game. If Brittany had responded with the opposite attitude, it would have cheated Jaz of her moment. On top of that, the rest of the team may have been unwilling to fully celebrate that moment had Brittany reacted differently to her situation. If Brittany had focused only on her own success and her own achievements, this story would not have been told. The most incredible part of this story isn't just Jaz's grand slam. This grand slam was a byproduct of her teammate's love and encouragement. I don't know if Jaz would have had the confidence to pull off that hit if Brittany hadn't been standing on the top step of that dugout, pouring every word of encouragement she had into Jaz's at bat. Brittany put her potential last collegiate at bat in Jaz's hands, and did so with confidence and eagerness for her teammate. That is what made this moment so unforgettable and so impactful. That is why these two will always be remembered. For this event is the epitome of what it means to be a teammate; starting with the remarkable amount of trust that was shown and completed by the unwavering support they shared.

There is a third character to this storyline that often goes unnoticed. One that did not end up on ESPN or talked about in the newspapers back home. However, her reaction to this now infamous grand slam was equally as amazing. Her name is Olivia Gibson. Olivia and Jaz both grew up in the Tuscaloosa area, home to the University of Alabama. They played side by side on the same travel ball team throughout their youth and when it came time to choose a college to finish their softball careers, the Alabama Crimson Tide was at the top of both their lists. Having been born and raised in Tuscaloosa, this would be a dream come true for both Jaz and Olivia. They both understood that Coach Murphy never before offered a spot on the team to two local girls in the same recruiting class. However this year, Murphy made an exception and Jaz and Olivia found themselves as teammates once again for the last four years of their softball careers. During the summer leading up to their first year as a member of the Crimson Tide softball team and throughout their freshman years they both worked tirelessly to find ways to better themselves so that they could in turn, better the team.

During that game on ESPN against Arizona State, it was quite obvious that everyone they both knew from back home would be watching the two Tuscaloosa girls compete for their hometown college team. Except when Murphy poked his head in the dugout, he could only choose one pinch hitter. And he chose Jaz, not Olivia. Olivia had worked just as hard. She had put in just as many hours of hitting and lifting and conditioning. Why hadn't she gotten the pinch-hit opportunity? Why couldn't it have been her to hit the grand slam? To get the texts and phone calls from home? How easy it would have been for all of these questions to cross Olivia's mind. When Jaz came back into the dugout after running head first into that celebration at home plate, she stumbled toward the bench with her hair a mess and her uniform disheveled from all the pats on the back, high fives, and fist bumps. Olivia greeted Jaz as she sat down to recuperate from her grand slam. Olivia was crying. Tears streamed down her face on which the biggest smile you have ever seen was plastered. She grabbed onto Jaz's shoulders and said, "Jaz! You did it! You did it!" She cried tears of joy. For her teammate. For her sister. Olivia felt Jaz's success with her, there was not a selfish tear that ran across her face that night.

Later that night at the hotel, Brittany was going through her luggage and gathering a change of clothes before her shower. We enjoyed celebrating Jaz's grand slam just a few hours earlier and were now in need of sleep before our games the next day. There were no ESPN cameras or microphones in our hotel room. Brittany paused for a moment, turned to me and said, "Jaz just became a legend! Can you believe what just happened? People are going to be talking about this forever, Cass! That was so amazing!" It truly was amazing. It was amazing what could happen when you had a team filled with athletes that showed such sincere joy for each other's triumphs.

It is a well-known fact throughout the program that any victory has a little bit of Brittany and the rest of the Alabama softball alumni a part of it. The foundation they laid for the rest of us, the values and traditions they took pride in passing down to each class was the cornerstone of why Alabama was successful that 2012 season.

The national player of year on the other team had made an adjustment from the night before and buried our batters 1-2-3 in the bottom of the first inning.

"Shake if off, shake if off."

"Hey time for 'D' Bama, time for 'D'."

"Let's go to work right here."

The chatter heard in our dugout was extremely helpful. Even in the 68th game of the season, our talk did not become background noise. Our encouragement to and from each other was able to help us all forget our past failures and stay in the present. There was nothing we could do about the past. We knew our brains were capable of time travel. Our mind had the ability of thinking about previous mistakes and eventually had the power to consume us. However, our body could not travel with our mind. Our body was stuck in the present. Therefore, in order to give ourselves the best chance for success, it was imperative that we all stayed where our body had no other choice than to be; in the present. There was no time to worry about what we couldn't control or worry about what could not be undone. The only time we had was now and we intended to constantly help each other stay there.

The second pitch of the top of the second inning was sent over the right field bleacher. Once contact was made with the pitch, my left ear that was closest to the opposition's dugout exploded. They knew it, we all did, right off the bat the ball was gone. They had the lead. Their team raced to home plate to greet their batter. Based on the noise, how loud the stands were, and how boisterous their dugout got it was obvious that Oklahoma believed they were going to win it.

"Hey, so what, Jackie? Let's win this pitch right here."

"I'm gonna pick you up right here Jack, I've got your back Jack."

"The next one, Jack! Get this next one!"

Our team members immediately began talking to Jackie in the circle. It doesn't feel good to give up a homerun and we all knew that. Staying silent during times of adversity is not the best plan of action for dealing with any difficult situation. It might feel like the natural thing to do, but the unnatural and difficult thing to do is to train yourself and your team to keep the talk loud. To remain positive and upbeat despite times when things are not going the team's way.

The next batter after the homerun reached on an error. 'Stop the bleeding,' was my first thought that came to mind. There were many times throughout the World Series Jackie could have gave in. Many times she could have said she was exhausted, that her body was pushed to it's max after already pitching 47 of the team's previous 67 games that year. But instead, she did something that you can't teach in a pitching lesson. Something you can't train in the weight room. Jackie got better when she was supposed to be fatigued. She became more difficult to hit when there were runners on base. She became untouchable when 'logic' said otherwise. She became determined, not frustrated and picked us up as a team when we needed it the most. She had that 'it' factor. After giving up a homerun and having a runner reach first base on an error, Jackie once again got better. Jackie got out of the inning with no more damage done.

Once again we sprinted off the field, determined to hit and get that run back. As we got back to the dugout, Kendall Dawson spoke up, "Hey, the team that has scored first every game has lost so far this series, right? So what that they scored first, there is a lot of time left, let's get it back right here." We got hyped in the dugout, energetic and enthusiastic about scoring this inning.

Once again, our hitters were retired 1-2-3. Reset, refocus, it was time for defense.

Their team led off the second inning with a hard base hit. After a fielder's choice and a ground ball back to the pitcher we found ourselves defending with a runner on second and two outs. Their number three batter came to the plate. She dug in to the batter's box and fixated her eyes on the ball our pitcher held in her hand just 43 feet away. Jackie delivered the pitch.

Once the ball left her bat, I tried to convince myself it would be a fly out to left field. I quickly realized that the ball was hit hard. Way too hard to be contained by the confines of the stadium. A two run home run for Oklahoma gave them a 3-0 lead in the final game of the national championship series. Once again, my left ear rang, their dugout came to life, their crowd boomed and they celebrated at home plate with victory on their mind. They were confident that they were going to win.

The next batter came to the plate. It was their number four batter, the batter that hit the homerun back in the second inning. After three straight balls, Coach Murphy stepped out of the third base dugout and called for a time out. He walked out to the mound as the rest of the infield hustled toward the pitching circle. Murphy put his arm around Kendall and leaned into the huddle, he was calm and he seemed to exude confidence in every word he spoke, "Hey, let's come back on this batter one pitch at a time, get back into the dugout, and score some runs."

Seemed like a great plan to me. We jogged back to our positions as Murphy walked back to the dugout. I could hear the crowd begin to rustle as they knew play was about to resume. One pitch, strike one.

"Atta girl, Jackie! Keep winning each pitch."

"Fight for it right here, Jack, fight for it!"

Second pitch, strike two. Our dugout got loud.

"Way to work, Jackie! Way to work!"

"I see you workin out there, Jack. Keep it up!"

"Hey, your best right here, Jack, your best! Let's get this one right here!"

Third pitch, strike three.

I yelled loudly but couldn't hear it. Our crowd went nuts. We sprinted off the field not like a team that was down by three but like a team that was playing with their heart. We didn't look like we were in a hole because not a single one of us was thinking about it. Our focus was on us and what we had to do. We had to play together and find a way to chip away and score some runs. We were playing for the love of the game, a team on a mission to win it all.

CHAPTER 10

"CELEBRATE THE DETAILS"

Monumental celebrations are usually following something that is well…monumental. The size of an accomplishment usually dictates the type of celebration a team will have on the field or court. However, something that is far less common to see is when a massive celebration follows what appears to be a small achievement.

There was one instance of this that involved teammate, Courtney Conley. Because of Courtney's work ethic and character she wasn't satisfied with just doing well, she was always determined to make her weaknesses even better. One season she had been struggling with taking the high pitch. Every day at practice we'd watch Court work on letting the high ball go with such diligence and precision. She wanted to get better at this in the worst way. This is a very small piece of an individual player's game yet, Courtney made sure to make even these small aspects just as important as the bigger ones.

One season, during the second game of a double header, Courtney Conley came to the plate in the second inning with no one on base and one out. We had already scored a few runs in the first and were feeling confident with our plan against the pitcher and team we were facing. The crowd was fairly quiet for a warm day in Tuscaloosa. Before Courtney came to the plate, Amanda Locke got everyone's attention in the dugout and said, "Hey, she's been working really hard on laying off that high pitch, when she actually does it in the game, let's celebrate with her."

On the third pitch of Courtney's at bat, in the bottom of that second inning, Courtney laid off a high pitch. Our dugout went *nuts*. The catcher for the other team caught the ball, slowly looked at our dugout, looked back at her pitcher, and shrugged her shoulders before finally throwing the ball back. The other team became so fascinated and focused on us that they forgot to talk to their pitcher. Everyone was trying to figure out what was going on. It was like they had just missed something monumental in the game. In an instant, our team's sole focus was on our teammate and her success and the opposing team's focus was now on *us* opposed to *their* teammate.

The smirk that came across Courtney's face as she took her next couple practice swings was unforgettable. Courtney didn't just appreciate our celebration of her take; she appreciated the fact that we were able to recognize the importance of her take. We were able to notice something she had been working on so diligently and were so proud when she finally accomplished it in a game. However, it is important to note that before we were able to celebrate that detail, we had *recognized* and *remembered* that detail first.

At my very first practice freshman year, Coach Murphy started off by saying, "We will not be the most talented team in the country."

'What?!' I thought to myself. This was by far the most talented group of people I had ever been around and the idea that there was potentially a more talented team out there scared my freshman self. He continued, "But, because we are going to pay attention to every detail, we will beat teams that may have more talent than us." The first thing we began to go over at that practice: how to grip a softball when we threw. No matter how small a detail seemed we made sure to go over it. Whether it was on the field, in the locker room, when studying film, or when introducing ourselves to people, our coaches made sure we were prepared for every element and left no rock unturned.

Every year on the last day of fall practice our coaches would play the, 'Pay Attention to Detail' game. We all knew it was coming yet when the day finally arrived it seemed to always shock and surprise us all. The team would be split into groups of two and were each handed a sheet of paper. Then the coaches would ask us questions regarding various details of family members names, guest speaker's names (with the correct spelling), details of the companies these guest speakers worked at, what the sign for a sacrifice bunt was, etc. The winner of this game usually got a fun prize. Although the stakes weren't incredibly high, don't forget, this team was extremely competitive. If we were competing at something, we were trying to win, bottom line.

The 'Pay Attention to Detail' game taught us the importance of noticing and remembering the small things. Not many people do this, so when you are able to remember someone's name after only meeting them once it really means a lot to them. When you can recall the message of a guest speaker months after the fact and not just minutes after the fact, it's usually a good indication the lesson in the message made a lasting impression.

Fast forward to the second game of the 2012 Women's College World Series. Our cleanup and power hitter, Amanda Locke found herself in one of the biggest slumps of her life. Since everyone on the team had been there before, we all knew that struggling at the plate could be a very lonely feeling. Playing at Alabama, softball is probably the one thing you as a player are best at. It is what you can relate to the most, what defines you. It's what you work your hardest at in order to perfect. When a player goes into a slump, especially a player who takes such pride in their hitting, it can be difficult to find a way out. Slumps are like quick sand, the more you try to maneuver your way out, the deeper you begin to sink.

Pressure mounts for different players in various ways. Pressure can come from the media incessantly focusing on every out, every strikeout, and every swing and miss. Or it can come from a parent, coach, or teammate doing the same. Pressure can also come from not wanting to let your teammates down. Regardless of where it comes from, internal pressure always begins with an outside source. Whether or not it manifests within you is dependent on you and you alone.

When Amanda Locke began her last playoff season of her career she wasn't playing the way she had wanted to be playing. Everyone on the team felt it, just as we celebrated in her successes, we sympathized in her struggles. During the first game of the World Series that year we played Tennessee and although Amanda didn't get her first hit of the playoffs, she did have better at bats and we all took notice. We kept reminding her to focus on the process (taking balls out of the zone, swinging at hittable balls in the zone) over the outcome (strikeout, groundout, fly out). This entailed celebrating a great at-bat when she took a ball or had a great swing at a strike but maybe just missed the ball with her bat. It was important for her to stay focused on the light at the end of the tunnel because no matter how bad it got, you knew you were always working toward it getting better.

In game two of the 2012 WCWS we played Arizona State and in Amanda's second at bat of the game she had a check swing infield single. Naturally, our dugout celebrated as if she had just hit a homerun. We felt her relief with her, we felt the pressure lift off of her shoulders, and we felt her walking lighter on her feet. That's all it takes; one time to have the tide turn. Later in the game, in the top of the sixth inning Amanda Locke was having an at-bat for the ages. She was battling pitch after pitch fouling off borderline balls with two strikes and finding a way to lay off of the pitcher's best pitch, a rise-ball.

During an at-bat like this, I absolutely loved being in the dugout. The dugout can be best compared to a jack in the box. Everyone knows the tune of this toy from his or her childhood. It is the tune that gets the child anxious in anticipation for the 'Jack' to pop out of the box. After several times cranking the toy, the child will begin to understand on what musical note the toy will pop up.

During each at-bat, everyone in the dugout had the utmost focus on the batter and is pouring everything they have into trying to get the hitter to succeed. The team is zoned in on celebrating the tiny details and visualizing the batter being victorious in their battle with the opposing pitcher. With each pitch the jack in the box cranks, the music plays and right as the pitch is mid-flight between the pitcher and the batter, there is a brief moment of silence where everyone holds their breath to see if 'Jack' pops out of his box. If the hitter takes the ball, there is a brief exhale in the dugout, the last note is left hanging and 'Jack' resets, remaining inside his box for the next pitch. Everyone in the dugout goes back to work. Praising their batter and doing everything in their power to figure out the edge needed in order to win the next pitch. That is really all this game is about, getting your mind right so your team can win one pitch at a time. When that much effort goes into every single pitch it becomes easy to celebrate the details with your teammates.

Leading up to that 3-2 count in Amanda Locke's at-bat, our dugout was busy at work, every single member taking pride in their specific job. The Arizona State pitcher stepped on the rubber and the music began to play. The jack in the box began to crank.

"Come on, Locke!"

The pitcher got the sign from her catcher and began her motion toward home plate.

"You're going to do it, Locke!"

The music started to pick up. Faster and faster it played, leading to the inevitable last note. That one note that made little kids stomach's flutter in anticipation.

"Win this pitch!"

The ball left the pitcher's hand and traveled in slow motion to home plate. Our dugout inhaled. The song was suspended, everyone in the stadium waited for the end result, waiting for that one, single note.

"*Pop.*"

The ball hit the bat. That was it, the last note we had been waiting for. Jack was out of the box and the dugout erupted with excitement. We watched the bright yellow ball soar off into the Oklahoma night sky and before it landed we were exploding onto the field.

Passionate chaos. That is the best way I can describe the way we celebrated. We ran up the steps and jumped over the dugout railing. We found anyway possible to get to home plate to greet our teammate, to make sure Amanda felt our excitement. Her slump was finally over, this was the light at the end of her tunnel. She just hit a homerun that gave us a lead in a pivotal World Series game. She found a way to be successful when it mattered the most. If you could see the smile that Amanda had when she rounded third base and trotted home you would understand her relief and her joy. You would understand the weight that had been lifted off her shoulders. I know we did because that feeling was there again, that feeling that can't be quantified. The one that you either have or you don't. Sure, any other team would have celebrated a go ahead homerun in the World Series. It was *how* we celebrated that mattered though. We were celebrating not just because of the homerun but because the weight had been lifted from our teammate, Amanda.

It is understandable why athletes feel exhausted after intense extra inning games or games where the stakes are higher. The athlete is mentally investing more of themselves with each and every pitch. If there are close to three hundred total pitches thrown in a game, this type of mental fatigue can wear on the team. In order to prevent debilitating exhaustion, there needs to be a release.

Some viewers of softball don't understand celebrating at home plate for each and every homerun. In baseball, when a player hits a homerun, he is greeted at the front of the dugout and only if his homerun was a walk off is he mauled at home plate by his fellow teammates. However, softball is different. None of us have a great chance at making softball our one and only job after college. This may have been it for us playing our sport. So, that crazy looking team at home plate that was waiting for Amanda Locke? That team that was jumping up and down, smiling, laughing, screaming, and cheering? That team that mobbed Amanda Locke and her smile of relief once she placed her foot on home plate? That's *my* team. Those are *my* teammates. I am filled with such pride from that one moment. It wasn't a pitching thing or a hitting thing or a coaching thing, it was all about the way we were able to celebrate.

If you are still playing don't ever take for granted an opportunity to celebrate with your teammates. It is something that you don't get to do often after your collegiate playing career is over. Actually, I haven't quite found an appropriate situation where screaming at the top of my lungs, fist pumping, jumping up and down, and slapping someone's helmet over and over again was acceptable after softball. Enjoy the opportunity to feel like you're five again. The coolest thing about any professional or collegiate team is when they get to celebrate. Just by watching how they enjoy themselves during moments of success will tell you a lot about the team. At the center of every team that exudes great chemistry is an awesome celebration that makes you smile just by watching.

We found ourselves hitting in the bottom of the third inning yet to have a Crimson Tide batter reach base safely. Amanda Locke stepped up to the plate for our team and beat out her second infield single of the World Series. Our dugout erupted once again and we celebrated that infield squibbler as if it were a hard hit shot in the gap. It was a tiny victory, but every detail no matter how small deserved a celebration. It was important to note that Amanda sprinted down the first base line at full speed. There was absolutely no excuse for a lack of hustle in our sport. It takes zero talent to have outstanding hustle, a great attitude, and put forth full effort. There is never an excuse to fall short in any of these categories. Locke sparked our team that night with our first hit and our first base runner of the game. We needed that because we needed something to get the ball rolling.

Early in a game against a great pitcher, it is imperative to find a way as an offense to make the opposing pitcher work. Although we didn't score or get on base in the first few innings, we knew every time we battled in an at-bat, we were successful. We challenged ourselves to redefine success. Success was not an outcome. The definition of success did not include doubles or homeruns. Success was giving our best effort no matter the situation. It was finding a way to be productive and help build toward the ultimate goal of winning this game.

Any time someone later in the lineup was productive after us, we realized that our contributions to wearing down the pitcher earlier in the game helped our teammates future at-bat. The game was all about constantly battling to find a way to tip the scales one grain at a time in our favor. The more pitches we saw as a team, the more the scales began to tip.

Although we didn't score in that third inning, we made adjustments. We found ways to put the ball in play. We found ways to make their pitcher and defense work harder. We knew with each pitch, we were chipping away at a dam. With each ball put in play we were removing a block from that dam. Maybe at first the water only trickled out, but we knew it was only a matter of time before the right block was removed and a huge flood of water broke through. After that third inning, even with the score still being 3-0, we could feel the pressure mounting and building. The dam was about to burst.

The first batter of the fourth inning for Oklahoma hit a shot toward right center field. Right fielder, Jazlyn Lunceford had a great read off the bat and ran the ball down in the gap. An out was an out, it didn't matter how hard it was hit. As the ball sailed back toward the infield from Jaz's hand, I felt a sprinkle hit my nose. I looked up in the direction of the lights and saw that it had began to rain again.

Jackie Traina walked the next batter on four straight balls. In the back of my mind I wondered if the rain had made the ball slick and difficult for her to control.

"Hey so what, Jack!"

"On to that next batter right here!"

"Let's win this one!"

The outpouring support from our teammates never ceased the entire game. It did not matter if we were losing, it did not matter if it was raining, we were in this together. It was always '20 on one' no matter the circumstance we found ourselves in.

The rain kept coming. Harder now than just moments ago. If the rain was affecting the way Jackie pitched, she would have to make an adjustment…quickly.

Jackie threw her fifth straight ball to the next hitter.

"Here we go, Jack! Keep fighting!"

The next pitch was a strike that made a loud 'smack!' as it hit Kendall's glove. Jack was adjusting. She kept rubbing the bright yellow ball against the side of her jersey in an attempt to keep it dry. The rain continued to fall.

With a 3-2 count, the number seven hitter for Oklahoma hit a hard shot to third baseman Courtney Conley. I could hear Jackie cheering for her infielder the entire play. Courtney was ready for it, she wanted every pitch to come her way and was anticipating that ball long before it ever left Jackie's hand. She snagged the hard shot and threw a bullet to second baseman, Danae Hays who quickly turned and whipped it to first base. Too late for a double play but we got the lead out which was important. Our infield pointed to Courtney, "Atta girl, Court!" Jackie pounded her glove in celebration and appreciated the support behind her as well.

With two outs and a runner on first, again Jackie walked the next batter on four straight balls. There are so many battles to fight throughout the course of a game. As a competitor you are never just battling the opponent, there is a constant struggle with other 'enemies.' These enemies can be anything from an inconsistent umpire, loud fans, or the weather. All of these things are well out of our control as athletes. We cannot ask the umpire to change the way he or she is calling balls and strikes, we cannot quiet a loud stadium, and we cannot ask the rain to stop or the temperature to change. Instead, we adjust. Just as we had trained our body in the weight room and on the field for ten months, we took advantage of every opportunity to train our mind. It made us mentally strong and fit to handle any situation thrown our way.

With two outs and runners on first and second, Jackie placed her feet on the mound and stared down at our catcher for the sign. She was not rattled or scared, she was ready. First pitch, strike one.

"Way to start it, Jack!"

Second pitch, ball one.

"Hey, so what, so what. On to the next one, Jack!"

"Innies let's get the easy force!"

"Outfield shooting home!"

Third pitch, strike two.

"Way to work, Jack!"

"I see you, Jack. Staying strong right here!"

Fourth pitch, ball two.

"Win it, Jack! Here we go 33, find a way to finish it!"

With two strikes our fans would get loud with the 'two strike clap' cheer. The fans would start to clap slowly as Jackie stood on the rubber and looked for her sign, and then the clapping got faster and louder until the pitch was finally released. However, with a 2-2 count and two outs, the dugout did not participate in the 'two-strike clap.' I could hear the managers and trainers yell, "Deuces!" from the dugout. They began rubbing the side of their hats; others without hats would motion with their hands as if they were rolling dice. Once the pitch was released dugout members would either remove their hat or release the imaginary dice from their hand. It may not make much sense but it was tradition. And you don't break tradition. Especially during the National Championship game.

As the claps from the stands got louder and louder, Jackie delivered pitch number five to the batter. A devastating change-up fooled the hitter as she swung right over the top of the ball. Strike three. Once again, Jack got better as the pressure mounted. I'm not quite sure how to describe or perfectly define what Jackie had that made her so successful during times like these. I was just thankful that Jackie had it, a whole lot of it.

CHAPTER 11

"IT IS A PRIVILEGE TO
WEAR THE JERSEY."

At one of the first practices of that 2012 season, the coaches had us meet in our film room prior to getting started on the field. The projector was set up and we all sat at our desks excited for what we were about to watch. Although none of us knew exactly what was going to be displayed on the screen in the coming moments, we knew based on previous videos this would be a good one. Anything the coaches projected on that screen always found a way to inspire us, give us perspective, and motivate us.

The video for that day was a speech given by Michigan State's quarterback Kirk Cousins at a Big 10 banquet. Our coaches thought this was a perfect video for us as athletes to see. After the video was complete, our team could not agree more with everything he said. Cousins spoke of it being a privilege to be an athlete. It was a privilege to play in the Big 10, to live his dream, to play in front packed stadiums, to be televised, have media want to interview him, and a humbling privilege to have fans pursue him for his autograph.

Throughout my four years at Alabama our coaches would preach to us day in and day out about how awesome of a blessing it was to be an athlete at Alabama. We got to continue playing our sport at one of the highest levels possible. What an extraordinary opportunity this was for each and every one of us. At one point or another we were all guilty of losing sight of perspective. We would maybe complain every now and then about the long hours that came with being an athlete; the early morning workouts, the aching bodies, or the hour and a half autograph session after playing a double header.

Perhaps we would compare our lives to those students that were non-athletes. Most college students can have a social life, worry free of making a mistake on a weekend and representing their team in a negative way. It was tempting to let our minds wonder about all the time we would have to complete school work had we not had long training sessions throughout the day. Listening to Kirk Cousins speech that day gave us all yet another tool to battle a bad perspective.

Being a student athlete was not a burden, it was a privilege. Missing out on a spring break trip at the beach because we had practices and games was not a missed opportunity. Instead, it was an honor to play this game and represent our university. Signing autographs was not a chore. It was an amazing chance to interact with fans that paid to watch us play and looked up to us with pride. Getting recognized and noticed at the local grocery store was not an inconvenience; it was a remarkable compliment and *privilege*.

This all goes back to a 'have to' vs. 'get to' vs. 'want to' attitude. When we woke up for weights at 5:00 am three days a week we challenged ourselves to rewire our mental thought process. Instead of saying, "I have to get up for weights right now," we tried to change it to "I get to wake up for weights right now." It was a chance of a lifetime to have something bigger than us to wake up for and to wake up as a member of the Crimson Tide Softball Team. It was a privilege to work out in one of the best facilities in the nation at the University of Alabama and a privilege to get trained by one of the best strength and conditioning coaches, Michelle Diltz. After just a short time of changing the 'have to' to a 'get to' we started to realize it actually turned into a 'want to.' We wanted to win a national championship and in order to do so, we needed to get better and we needed to be at our best when it mattered the most. Therefore, we wanted to wake up for weights. We wanted to sign autographs, volunteer and make a difference, go to class to get an education, and take advantage of every opportunity to make ourselves the best person, athlete, and softball player we could be.

In the spring of 2012, Coach Murphy brought a large cardboard box with him to practice. He grabbed the first crimson t-shirt at the top of the box and held it up for our team to see. In white lettering, the shirt read, 'Alabama Softball, A PRIVILEGE to wear the jersey.' We were very thankful for that gift and I think it soon became a lot of our favorite practice shirts. How special it truly was to wear the jersey. Hall of Fame baseball player, Roberto Clemente once said, "When I put on my uniform, I feel I am the proudest man on Earth."

The uniform held all of us to a much higher standard. "Whom much is given, much is expected in return" was a common saying throughout the program. The 'much' that was 'expected in return' however, was not homeruns and stolen bases. The 'much' that was expected of us consisted of the team acting with dignity and class in everything we did. It meant appreciating the opportunities given to us on a daily basis.

"You're never going to know how good you have it here until you don't have it anymore." Coach Murphy used to say this to us a lot. I thought I knew what he was talking about. I thought he meant that we should try and appreciate everything we had been given; the cool Nike gear, the amazing facilities, and the scholarship money that paid for our education. It wasn't until I left the game that I realized how rare it was to have a catch with a good friend, how pretty the grass and dirt looked side by side, or the sweet smell of a leather glove.

I don't believe there is any way to completely erase these feelings but there are certain ways to lessen the blow that an athlete feels once their eligibility is up. It is all about being able to take advantage of the time we have to wear the jersey and play. It is a challenge to take a step back and realize how blessed we were to be standing on a softball field, in a jersey, while representing our team, school, family, and hometown. The opportunity to do all these things *was a privilege*.

In May of 2012 on my class's senior day, fellow senior, Kendall Dawson posted a tweet that really stuck out to me. It read, "After four amazing years, today is my last time to step on our field with a #12 on. Going to make the best of it because it's made the best of me." Isn't that the point of any sport? You put your head down, give everything you have to the game and when it is all said and done the game of softball leaves you the best version of yourself you could be. It is an honor to play this sport and I could not imagine playing it any other place aside from at the University of Alabama.

I was fortunate enough to know when the last time I'd wear my jersey would be. After that final game of the 2012 World Series, it was late and we had to get back to the hotel, shower, pack, and get ready for our flight back to Tuscaloosa the following morning. While my sophomore roommate, Ryan, changed and showered fairly quickly, I took my time. I decided to clean the hotel room up a little bit, unpack all my clothes, fold them, and then repack them again. All the while I remained in my smelly, muddy uniform.

Around 5:00 am Ryan looked at me with a smile and said, "Cass, you really gotta go shower now." I knew I did, it was something I had been dreading for four years: Taking the jersey off knowing I'd never put it back on again. I took one good long look in the mirror and I'll never forget it because I was so disheveled. I had one sock on and one sock off from when I had to cut the athletic tape off my ankle. My uniform was unbuttoned and half tucked in and half tucked out. My face had one eye black on and one eye black off. The right eye black had been somehow wiped away. My pants were filthy with mud and dirt from *that* iconic Hall of Fame Stadium. To top it all off, my hair was an absolute mess. However, I wouldn't have wanted it any other way. It was one of those moments I didn't need a camera for to remember forever.

"CASS! Just wanted to send you a little reminder that we are SO happy that you wear crimson and white!" I still have some of Coach Aly's text messages saved that she would randomly send out throughout my career. She never failed to make us all feel appreciated. She was also very good at reminding us that no matter the struggle or adversity we may have been facing, what we had at Alabama was an enormous privilege. There were hundreds, if not thousands, of people who would love to have been in our shoes as a student athlete. It was a privilege to be surrounded by such amazing people on a daily basis. It was a privilege be a part of something bigger than us. A privilege to carry on the tradition laid out by so many who came before us. It was a privilege to wear the jersey.

"Yeah, Bama! Yeah, Bama!"

We sprinted off that field ready to hit. We were ready to once and for all shatter the last brick holding this dam together. We were ready for the dam to burst. Our three, four, and five hitters were set to come to the plate for us in the bottom of the inning and our excitement was evident. Murphy came into the huddle, got our attention, and explained to us the plan. We were going to need to make an adjustment if we were going to be successful in this game. We had a new game plan to follow and we all nodded our heads in agreement as Coach Murphy spoke, simultaneously buying in. No one questioned it or doubted it. Murphy delivered the plan in a clear, concise, and confident manner. Best of all, he was calm. If there was any panic within him he didn't let it show and that helped us more than anything else. It all starts at the top.

"Boomer!" "Sooner!"

The Oklahoma faithful felt they were only twelve outs away from a national title and were getting loud with their cheers in the stands. It appeared the rain had emptied some of the seats for the Oklahoma fans which was understandable. It was getting late and these fans that lived nearby would have a dry place to go watch the game. Our fan base consisted of our families, close friends, and fans that traveled from all over the country. They had nowhere to go because the only place they would have wanted to be would be right here in Hall of Fame Stadium, cheering in the rain for the Alabama Softball team. That was a special feeling.

Their pitcher got into the circle for Oklahoma to begin the fourth inning. She had five strikeouts, two hits, and had thrown just 43 pitches up until that point. We needed to make her work more, that was obvious to all of us. Kaila Hunt, our number three hitter, stepped up to the plate for her second at-bat of the night. The rain still continued to fall from the Oklahoma night sky.

The first pitch of the at-bat landed way off the mark in the dirt for ball one. I thought to myself, 'I wonder how well she can throw in the rain.' The second pitch missed the strike zone again, ball two. This time I said it out loud, "Hey, she doesn't look like she likes the rain..." Just as ball three was delivered to Kaila Hunt a teammate grabbed my arm and agreeably exclaimed, "She can't throw in the rain!"

"Let's get loud!"

Our dugout erupted. It was as if I could feel the water trickling from the dam. 'One more brick.' I thought to myself. 'Just one more brick and this thing is going to blow.'

Two pitches later I heard a noise come from Kaila Hunt's bat that our team hadn't heard all night. The ball connected with the barrel of Kaila's bat perfectly and ricocheted past a diving shortstop into left field for a hard hit single. Our dugout went nuts. Our stands erupted. That is exactly what we needed. The dam was about burst, I just knew it. I could feel it.

A wild pitch got Kaila Hunt to second base. After two straight outs we found ourselves with two outs and a runner still stranded 120 feet away from home plate. Kendall Dawson was the fourth batter to come to the plate for the Tide this inning. Another wild pitch advanced Kaila to third. Kendall was able to work a walk to give us runners on the corners with two outs and senior Amanda Locke stepping up to the plate.

"Here we go, Locker!" Our team was in the batter's box with Amanda. Her demeanor at the plate told me she could feel it, the power of '20 on one.' She wasn't having to do this alone, none of us were. The rain steadily continued to fall.

Wild pitch number three of the inning scored Kaila Hunt. If I thought our dugout got excited for one of our teammates taking a ball, *you should have seen us when we scored a run. I immediately heard the all too familiar drum roll of the Alabama fight song play across Hall of Fame stadium. We had cut the deficit to two runs. With Kendall advancing to second base on the wild pitch, we were still threatening despite the two outs.*

As I congratulated Kaila on a job well done, I noticed Amanda stepping away from the batter's box. The coaches and umpires were meeting behind home plate.

"It's not about the rain is it?" One teammate asked.

"The field is fine to run on, it's not slippery yet." Kaila Hunt pleaded. Momentum was on our side, this dam was about to flood, and the last thing we wanted right now was a rain delay. We wanted nothing more than to be on the field playing, to keep the Tide rolling.

"Hey, Jackie had to pitch in this, too! It's not raining any harder now than before!" A supportive Bama fan yelled from the stands.

Coach Murphy walked back from behind home plate as their team jogged off the field and into their dugout. We were in another delay.

CHAPTER 12

"EARNED NOT GIVEN."

"**H**ey! How heavy is it?!"

It's amazing the high you can get from a workout. Our team would drag our feet into the weight room at 5:30 am for 6:00 am workouts. Especially on those cold mornings it was obvious some of us had a hard time getting out of bed. Eyes slightly swollen from having an alarm disrupt our REM cycle, hair a mess, and clothes wrinkled. Yet, something happened about half way through workouts. From being an exercise science major I knew the physiological reason for our 'workout high.' Once workouts begin, endorphins in the body are released, and the result is feelings of euphoria and reduced stress.

It seemed that no matter how difficult the workout would be, there would be some point in which we would get excited. We would realize what we were doing; we were training for a national championship. We were making payments toward that trophy that was waiting for us in Oklahoma. That is exciting stuff!

As I jogged from one station to the next across the weight room, in between breaths I kept asking my teammates, "How heavy do you think it is?!" Every now and then I would hear Amanda Locke reply with, "I bet it's real heavy, Cass!"

I was talking about the trophy. The stained wooden trophy with the gold NCAA seal across the top. The trophy with the engraved lettering "2012 National Champions." I wanted to know how heavy that trophy was. I'm not sure when it began but I would start talking about playoffs during workouts. During the difficult leg circuits or what felt like the endless sprints on the turf. I never wanted to deter focus from our present task at hand, but I did know that the future would provide motivation. It would be a good reminder of why we were here, giving everything we had, even when we felt like we didn't have anymore to give.

Some of the best team memories I have is getting fired up in the weight room at 6:30 am. You know how cool it is to cheer your teammate on as they hit a new personal record on squat? Or when they are fighting to get a bar up on bench press and by the team yelling "Let's go!" they find a way with shaking arms to press the bar straight up. There is something special about those team work outs because the team *wants* to be in the weight room. They *want* to get up early and get their work in. They might not always like it, but it's what they *want*. Because what we wanted most as a team, was to be the best team we were capable of being. We knew if we did that, if we accomplished our potential, then there would be no team that could beat us. We trained to not just beat our opponent, but to make them quit. We wanted them to be miserable when they played us. Watching everyone jump on board with this idea is fun. It's exciting. And it's extremely special.

I began assigning playoff games for workouts. If we had five leg circuits to do, I would assign a World Series game to each circuit. During one particular workout, freshman, Danielle Richard was completing her squats. I began to talk to her about what I thought that game of the 2012 WCWS would be like in six months. What uniforms we would wear, what the crowd would sound like, what the feeling would be like after we won. Being a senior, I did most of the talking for the first few weeks of training in the fall. On one particular Friday morning, I started my second leg circuit and heard Danielle say, "So, how many homeruns you think we're gonna hit in the second game?" That most definitely made me smile. To an outsider watching, I was probably smiling too big for the hurting my legs were taking.

I liked doing this for two reasons. First, whenever you are training for something, instead of dwelling on how difficult the workout is, it's nice to be distracted from the strain in your muscles and how out of breath you really are. The mind will be able to push your limbs so much further than your body ever thought possible. Secondly, I think every team who has a goal needs to talk about it. You want to win the conference championship, state title, or national title? It better be a well-known goal. You need a road map of things you as a team can control in order to get there. A goal without a plan just floats in space. You can hope for it and wish for it, but in order to make it a possibility you must work for it.

Kayla Braud told me one day that she likes to practice like she's the worst player on the team. This might sound strange coming from an All-American. Her mentality transcended to the rest of us. She was one of the best and she never stopped trying to find ways to make herself better. Therefore, we made a commitment to practice like the worst team. We never wanted to settle. We never wanted to think we made it. We never wanted to think we didn't need to get better. Imagine if you were the worst player on the team. How many things would you work on in order to improve? Probably everything. It is a never-ending relentless pursuit for greatness when you have an opportunity to make your dreams a reality. Every practice we'd hustle and push like we were the worst, but always played in games with the confidence like we were the best.

Before practices would start, some of us would write one physical goal and one mental goal on an index card and stick it in our back pocket of our practice pants. This way, no matter how hectic practice may have gotten, we always had a reminder of what we were focusing on getting better at that day. After a while, those cards added up to a pretty big stack of things you improved on. That stack of index cards became something we were really proud of.

Our volunteer assistant coach that year, Adam, was from Ann Arbor, Michigan and was a huge asset to helping us improve in 2012. He gave us a great motto for our season. I can remember him walking in front of the team in our meeting room and telling us this story about something he'd like to purchase in June. "Now this item is very, very expensive. We're not going to be able to pay for it all at once come June. So, we're going to have to make some payments throughout the year." He went on to explain that every time we give full effort in the weight room, every time we went all out in practice, anytime we hit or fielded extra, we were making a payment. "If you paid for something, there isn't a doubt in your mind that it is yours. So when we get to Oklahoma in June, we're just going to pick up what is rightfully ours." I got chills when he said it, *rightfully ours*.

There is no way to tell if you are the hardest working team in the country. You don't have eyes and ears at every practice facility or every weight room. The focus of hard work cannot be compared to anyone else but yourself. The definition of working your hardest is giving everything you have in your tank that day. Sure, there are going to be days when you are sore, tired, fatigued and maybe your tank is at only half full. But you know what? You must be willing to give all of that 50% in order to achieve that one thing you want most. That's how you get better every single day.

There are only 365 days in a year. Which means you can only get 365 days better in a year. When you go to bed at night, you have to ask yourself a difficult question and answer truthfully. Did I get better today? Can I say I made a payment today for something I want in the future? If the answer is no, then you can never make that day up again. You can't get two days better tomorrow. You can only get one day better each day! We made a commitment that year to finding a way to make each day better than the day before. We knew that when we woke up in the morning, that day was either going to be better or worse than the day before, but it would never be the same. The only person responsible for making that decision was you.

It's easy to cut corners and take the smoothly paved road with less bumps and hills along the way. It's easy to not ask yourself the tough questions at the end of the day. But here's the thing, when you don't complete the right number of sets, or when you don't empty your tank on any given day, your parents won't find out. Your coaches and teammates might not even find out. But you know who will know? You. You and the game. Because the game knows. The game knows who gave their all on that diving play, who ran extra, who worked on their weaknesses, and who put the hours in. And the game will reward you.

This is what makes our sport so special to us. It wasn't, 'just a game,' it was our life. What our fans saw on the field was merely the tiny tip to an iceberg of enormous proportions. The end result was the culmination of hard work, passion, and desire from so many workouts, practices, and games prior to that. This is what makes it hurt so badly when the desired end result doesn't happen. It's why losing keeps us up at night and why the one play we didn't make is the first thing we think about the morning after. It is the reason we cry when it's all over. If this was 'just a game' we probably wouldn't sit in silence on the bus rides home. Rather, we would probably be able to laugh and go out to dinner afterwards as if nothing was wrong. No, this wasn't 'just a game,' this was our *life*. We committed our time to this. We sacrificed our bodies beyond belief for this. However, this is also why winning felt so sweet. Why we can't explain to other people just how special the celebrations were. It is difficult to understand these feelings without experiencing it to the extent we have. It is difficult to understand why the struggles were always worth it.

When you are committed to something, you are all in. That is the only way to do it. When you are committed, then the morning weights, the hours spent conditioning in the scorching heat, and the four-hour practices don't seem so bad. They end up being what you want, because when you are committed to achieving something, you are more than willing to give every fiber of your being for it.

The bottom line was that we wanted to *earn* our wins. We were humbled in October of 2011 when we played our first game together of the fall season and got beat pretty badly by a team that was not expected to be victorious. However, I am extremely thankful for that loss, despite it not feeling very good at the time. It reinforced the idea of earning victories and that nothing would be handed to us. If it were that easy then a lot more people would be doing it. But there were only twenty people that were selected for the task. Twenty people that were chosen to play for this team. Coach Murphy always said the best way to respect an opponent was to beat them. By beating them, you let them know you gave them your best. You never acted or played as if you'd win just by showing up; you had to give your best and work for it regardless of the opponent. Anything less than our best would be disrespectful. Not just to the other team but to our teammates, coaches, families, alumni, university, and finally to the game. I cannot say it enough, *the game knows*. The game knows when you cut corners and the game knows when you only gave half of your tank. The game knows how many days out of the year you got better. When it came time for our national title game on June 6, 2012 we were confident, we were calm, and we were focused. Not because of what we were going to do on that one night but because of what we had done in the days, months, and years leading up to that single game. We knew what we had given, and even better than that, we knew that the game had been paying attention.

I mentioned earlier that we had dealt with a lot of adversity that year. Our coaches took another job in the SEC and then returned to Alabama. Our beloved trainer, Addy had made her trip to heaven sooner than any of us anticipated. We had dealt with injuries, losses, slumps, crazy travel plans gone wrong, and much more. There was no way a little rain was going to discourage us nor stop our momentum.

During the delay, the Oklahoma team did what probably looked like the smart thing to do. They sat inside the confines of their dugout and remained dry in order to rest and preserve their energy. They did exactly what 'logic' told you to do. However, our team jumped out of the dugout and stood on the field in the rain. We began cheering with our fans.

"Ala!" Our team would exclaim.

"Bama!" The stands replied with great fervor.

If anyone turned the television on during that delay and saw the way we were cheering and laughing, I don't think they would have guessed we were down 3-1 in the 4ᵗʰ inning.

"I said it's great to be from Ala-Bama!"

We were losing our voices with each yell but we didn't care. This was it for us, this was the final game, we were stuck in the present and enjoying every second of it.

One after another we came up with some cheer or some chant to keep momentum with us. Our number one fan, Emily Pitek Clifford, led the way the entire time. Her arms waved and instructed the Bama faithful as well as any conductor could have done with their orchestra. Just as each player had a specific role and job to do, so did our fans. And just like the players, our fans did their job to the best of their ability with maximum effort.

Our focus during this rain delay was on us. On our team. Our family. That was all we cared about. We didn't care about the weather, the umpires, the T.V. cameras, or the other team. We just cared about us. There was nothing that could take our focus away from what was the most important thing to us at that point in time. It was so special and it was something we all felt.

Jackie Traina sat in the dugout and rested her legs. Teammate Lauren Sewell braided her hair as they laughed and cheered along with the rest of the team. Jackie wasn't concerned about the three runs she had given up because she knew there was absolutely nothing she could about that. She couldn't go back in time and change any of it. All she could do was get herself ready for what she had to do for the remainder of the game and put her faith in the rest of the team to win us back the upper hand. We were relaxed and having fun. Is that not the best way to play this game? With passion, enthusiasm, and pure joy? There was no room for doubt or fear. Instead, we were in the cage with fear and we were dancing with it.

Our team huddled up in the rain outside the dugout. With our arms around one another we swayed back and forth with huge smiles on our face. How rare is that? How special of an opportunity is that? To have so many of those you care about surrounding you. People who understood fully what you had gone through in order to get to that point because they never left your side.

"Hey! Hey!" Courtney Conley yelled into the huddle to get everyone's attention.

"We sink! We swim!" She started…

The rest of the team chimed in without hesitation, "We rise! We fall! We meet our fate together!" We were all quoting one of the motivational videos we had just watched hours earlier on the bus ride over to the game.

After about thirteen minutes the umpires walked back out onto the field. Following a brief meeting with the coaches, we had found out we were going to begin play again. Just like when we were younger, we were about to head home for the night when darkness fell. It was as if the lights had flickered back on again, extending our playtime into the night. The lights wouldn't go out on our season just yet. We were so ready to play. Our intensity had remained where it needed to be in order to continue chipping away at the dam. Our team got back into position.

"Hey, Locke!" Before taking her spot on second base, Kendall Dawson ran over to talk to Amanda Locke before her at-bat. "You can hit the ball anywhere to the outfield and you know I'll score because I'm so fast." Kendall had a big smile on her face as she said this. It was a comical statement considering Kendall was cursed with catcher's running speed.

CHAPTER 13

"IF YOU SURROUND YOURSELF WITH GOOD PEOPLE, GOOD THINGS WILL HAPPEN."

The title of this chapter will hold true not just for a team but also for a company, a family, or anyone's life. If you are able to fill your days with good people then good things are headed your way. It may be a day, a week, or a year but eventually so much good will come from the people you keep close by your side. From a softball team's stand point, I also believe the opposite can be true. Our coaches preached day in and day out that we were hand selected to be a part of this team because they felt we were a perfect fit for this program. Our coaches would pass on talent if there were character flaws in a recruit. They firmly believed that a player who was a better person at their core was going to be more beneficial to the team than someone with talent alone. When they say, "beneficial to the team" they are not necessarily referring to the win and loss column. Success can be described in many different ways. There is only one person that determines your definition of the word and that's you.

Our season was a marathon and not a sprint. We played 68 games during the 2012 season. Out of the 365 days in a year we spent roughly 257 of them with each other. We didn't need to have something softball scheduled to find ourselves hanging out together. During breaks from school, teammates would visit one another to see each other's families and hometowns. This was a special group of people we had at Alabama. I firmly believe that each and every one of us were better people than softball players, better people than coaches, and better people than trainers or managers. We strove to be great people first, and good players second. We genuinely cared about one another and that mattered a lot to all of us.

Our journey was what was important. As I look back and remember the practices and games, I notice that with each passing year the memories get a little less well defined. Little by little the details fall out of focus and the memories become more obscure than clear. However, the memories that I can replay in my mind with crystal clear recollection are the times we were having fun together. The ever entertaining stories that we will tell at team reunions for years to come. Of course winning a national championship would be a great feeling, but it would be an even better feeling if we won it with the right people. If you spend close to seventy percent of your year with a group of people and don't enjoy the journey, then does the end result even matter?

I would tell recruits all the time that there were many places they could go to college, earn a degree, and play softball. Numerous institutions offered that. However, there were far fewer places they could go where their success on the field wouldn't determine whether or not they would enjoy their college experience. I often say to people, I wouldn't have to win the last game of my career for my duration at Alabama to be the best four years of my life. The end result wouldn't be the main focus. Instead, we as a team would make the effort to enjoy the journey and the process. And as a result, the happy ending would hopefully take care of itself.

I once spoke with my coaches about recruiting. It always seemed like they had their finger on the pulse of someone's character. Just by having a conversation with the prospect they would know right away if they were going to be a good 'fit' for the program. One characteristic that really stuck out to me was how respectful a recruit is to their parents. A player once gave her mom lip about getting her the wrong Gatorade flavor. That was it for my coaches, they knew right away. Despite a 4-4 performance with 2 homeruns and a stolen base, she just wouldn't fit. Our coaches would always say, "If they don't treat their parents with respect, they're never going to treat us with respect."

Without fail every year our coaches would always find a reason to thank us. There would be a headline about an athlete from across the country getting a DUI, another athlete who was academically ineligible, or some player who got into a fight at a bar. Our coaches would stand up in front of the team and thank us for always doing the right thing. In reality, we should have been the ones thanking them. They were the ones responsible for recruiting us, bringing us together to the same place, at the same time, introducing us, and making us better. They were the ones that had fit the puzzle pieces together. They hand picked girls with strong minds, righteous morals, and tough hearts who fit the bill. They constantly thanked our parents for how hard they had worked to give us solid foundations on which great athletes could be built.

Every athlete has extraordinary potential. However, it is not just their talent that allows them to reach this ceiling of possibility. A player must possess both the discipline and character to guard their talent along with the work ethic to develop it. Several coaches will tell you they will take the less talented player in high school with the enormous heart versus the highly talented player with character flaws and an unwillingness to develop their mental game. The player with heart will not stop once they have given it their all. They will keep working until they get better. Then in turn, they will help develop and create an environment conducive to producing champions. They will become a perfect blueprint for others to look up to and help set an example that demands bringing out the best in each person as a human being as well as a player.

During the fall of my senior year at the very end of practice Coach Murphy called us into a huddle.

"I have a challenge for you all."

Our eyes got wide with anticipation. Would this be a hitting challenge? Bunting challenge? Defensive challenge?

"For 21 days straight, I want you all to find a way to make someone's day."

I saw a big smile spread across everyone's face in that huddle. This was a challenge that was certainly not softball related as we may have anticipated. I could tell my teammates were already racking their brain about who's day they were planning on making over the next month or so.

Coach Murphy gave us an example of 'paying it forward.' The other night he had been at the drive-thru to get dinner. He told the woman at the window as he went to pay that he would like to pay for the car behind him as well.

"Do you know the car behind you?" Asked the woman at the window.

"No, just something I wanted to do." Replied Murphy.

The woman at the window responded, "Well just for that I'm gonna give you an extra large soda because you seem like such a good person."

Needless to say, when you surround yourself with good people, you're going to feel pretty full day in and day out. That is exactly what Coach Murphy intended to do when he hired his coaching staff. Exactly what our coaches did when they hired our managers, trainers, and support staff. Exactly what they did when they recruited all of us. Even on my worst days I couldn't help but look at my teammates and coaches that surrounded me and feel extraordinarily lucky.

If you find yourself on a team, in a relationship, or even at a job where you feel that the people around you are not making you better, it is probably a good idea to change something in your life. A lot of people I know stay at a job they hate with a boss that treats them poorly because they are making a lot of money. At the end of the day, is it worth it?

Every year there is an end of the year banquet dedicated to the seniors. Throughout the night, each senior gets up to the podium and they all have something to say to everyone within the organization. One of my favorite speeches came from Whitney Larsen. She had a piece of paper outlining what she had intended to say and used it to thank our team, the doctors, trainers, strength coaches, managers for everything they had done to help her throughout her career. She had a very heartfelt thank you to her family and then finally, she got to the coaches. She tossed the paper to the side and paused a second to compose herself.

"Leaving here, I can honestly say you coaches have made me the best possible version of my myself that I could be."

That one quote echoed loudly for me because it carried with it the weight of so much truth. There are going to be many paths that present themselves to you in your life. Everyday, each decision you make determines which path you will choose to travel. Ask yourself which path makes you the best 'you.' Which path is lined with people that hold you to a higher standard day in and day out? Which path challenges you and elevates you to demand the best out of yourself?

On June 3, 2012 we were warming up and all set to play against the number one seeded California Bears. It was semi-final Sunday at the Women's College World Series and as the day went on the temperatures continued to rise. We needed one win to advance to the championship series. We had been in that exact position the year before and instead of getting our one win we were beat twice by the same team and were sent packing for Tuscaloosa. This was not something we liked to remember and definitely not something we wanted to repeat.

We finished our warm up routine and jogged toward each other for our pre-game huddle. Senior Kendall Dawson leaned forward into the huddle just a little bit. She didn't have her sunglasses on and I could see her eyes scan the faces of our team as she looked at each and every one of us. She looked calm and confident. As our catcher, she was the one person everybody on the field was facing toward. Throughout the season she always seemed to provide a calming presence for us all to look to. Kendall began, "I was saying my prayers last night...and thought of each person on our team."

I felt myself start to smile. Kendall's voice started to quiver just a little bit; she wasn't a fan of public speaking, which is unfortunate because every time she spoke, our team listened very intently. Maybe it was because she didn't always have much to say or maybe it was because when she did speak, it was always very valuable.

Kendall continued, "As I went down the list of everyone's name on our team, I realized clear as day that each and every one of us are good people. And we deserve this. Each and every one of us deserves this. So there shouldn't be a doubt in anyone's mind that good things should happen to us." There were nods from the entire huddle. If we were going to win this thing, it was going to be with the right group of people, each one of us deserving of the amazing opportunity to stand in this huddle with the once in a lifetime chance of winning a national championship before us.

"Here we go. Locke!"

Amanda Locke had worked the count full in the first at-bat after following the rain delay. The rain hadn't completely stopped but definitely lessened since play was first suspended.

"Fight for it, Locke! Find a way to fight!"

Our dugout wouldn't stop cheering. I began to hear how hoarse our voices were getting. We were dialed in on Amanda's at-bat, as was Oklahoma's team. They wanted to stop the bleeding, we wanted it to hemorrhage. Amanda Locke delivered a clutch two out base hit to left field. The left fielder came up with the ball cleanly and fired it home as Coach Murphy windmilled his arm signaling Kendall Dawson for home plate.

"Go! Go!"

"Run, Kendall!"

I don't think your brain knows exactly what to say with that much excitement but something usually does come out of your mouth. Our dugout was trying to do everything possible to get Kendall to score. I'm sure if it were allowed you'd see teammates run out onto the field to push behind Kendall.

The throw was off and Kendall ran home safely. We cut the deficit to one. Amanda never stopped running from first and got herself into scoring position at second base. We were still threatening. We were still removing bricks from the dam and the water was finally flowing through.

The next batter up was Courtney Conley. The previous year Courtney had been practicing live hitting off of one of our pitchers. She had swung at a bad pitch, got frustrated at herself for swinging instead of taking the ball and as a result of the frustration swung at another bad pitch for strike three. One of the coaches let Courtney know that her frustration wasn't going to get her anywhere, there was no room for it, and something had to change for her to be successful. No one enjoys being told they did something wrong, it is not fun, and as a member of the team we had all been there multiple times before. There are several different ways to handle this, some better than others. That night Courtney texted our coach with a message that read, "I've been thinking about what you said about getting frustrated vs. getting determined. I'm going to be in the same situation in the national championship game and I will take that second pitch instead of swinging at it again. Thank you for making me better."

Well, if you watch Courtney's at bat in that fourth inning, she swings and misses at a ball early in the count. A smart pitcher will go back to that same spot later in the at-bat and that is exactly what Oklahoma's pitcher did. Except now, Courtney didn't bite. Courtney was determined. There was no room for frustration and she took the following pitch. I couldn't help but smile. She did exactly what she said she would do. She saw her success before it happened. On the 34th pitch of the inning, Courtney Conley hit a shot. The ball flew off the bat with such velocity straight to centerfield that it looked like it would clear the fence. Our entire team held their breath as we saw Oklahoma's center fielder retreat for the wall. She was in a full sprint as she stretched her glove arm out in an attempt to catch the ball. The ball barely cleared her glove and landed on the warning track. Amanda Locke sprinted home and Courtney slid safely into second base. Still threatening. The water was now gushing from the dam.

Volunteer assistant coach, Adam Arbour had to barricade the entrance of the dugout with his body so that we didn't fly out onto the field too soon to celebrate. Fist bumping, high fiving, jumping up and down, and passionate chaos ensued once we were released. We pointed and yelled for Courtney at second. What a hit! We tied the game, 4-4. But we were not satisfied yet. We didn't play to tie, we played to win and we had an opportunity for the lead.

"Now stepping to the plate, #2, Jazlyn Lunceford."

The announcer exclaimed across the stadium. It was like déjà vu all over again. "Hey now, is there anyone else you want at the plate at the World Series in a clutch situation?" I heard that comment come from a teammate at the end of the dugout and it got a couple laughs from the team. It was true. Jaz had a way of living for those clutch moments. It didn't always have to be a momentous pinch-hit grand slam but she always seemed to find a way to get it done when it mattered the most.

On the second pitch of Jaz's at bat, Jaz hit a wicked curve ball off the end of her bat that squibbled toward the shortstop. Jaz tore down the first base line. Despite what 'logic' said about the ball being a routine ground out, she was on a mission to give everything she had to beat that ball out. There was no such thing as a routine groundball, especially in a final game like this. Courtney Conley took off from second base with two outs and never once assumed an out would be recorded. She anticipated the worst-case scenario. She ran hard from the start. The throw from Oklahoma's shortstop went straight into the ground and got away from their first baseman. Coach Murphy never stopped waving Courtney around third. She rounded the bag and took off in a sprint for home.

"Go! Go! Go!"

I could hear the anticipation in our dugout. It was as if Courtney was running with all of us by her side. The first baseman recovered the ball and fired it across the diamond toward home. I don't have a scientific explanation for it but time slows down during these moments. What probably happened in a split second felt so much longer. I could feel our team collectively inhale and hold our breath as Courtney raced toward home trying to beat the throw coming from the right side of the field. The throw looked like it would beat her there. Court approached the catcher and dipped her left shoulder in an attempt to curve her body away from the tag. As she slid, she extended her left arm and *her fingertips slid across home plate as the ball got away from their catcher. Coach Murphy's right arm flew straight up into the air as he fist pumped in celebration.*

"Safe! Safe!"

We erupted. The dam was now exploding. Poor Adam couldn't hold us back. Courtney and Murphy embraced. We had the lead. We were in control of our destiny. Victory was in our collective sight. We couldn't help but feed off of one another.

Our next batter up attempted a bunt single down the third base line and was barely thrown out at first base to end the threat. However, the damage was already done. What an inning that was!

Any time a team has a big inning offensively, the main goal of the opposition is to try and create a similar outcome. Their job is try and find a way to get the runs back that the other team scored. The job of the now defensive team is to throw water on that fire and to not allow their comeback to be anything more. Our goal was to get off the field and back on offense as quickly as possible.

The first batter for Oklahoma hit a ground ball to Kaila Hunt at shortstop that was quickly fielded and thrown to first for out number one. The second batter hit a ground ball toward the middle of the field that was backhanded by second baseman Danae Hays and thrown to first for out number two. We were fired up with those quick two outs. Only seven more outs until we were champions, however I can guarantee you no one on our team was thinking that. We were zoned in to focusing on one inning at a time, one out at a time, and one pitch at a time.

The third batter of the inning walked. The fourth batter of the inning was hit by a pitch leading to runners on first and second with two outs and the number five batter for Oklahoma coming to the plate.

"No worries, Jack, no worries."

"On to the next one, Jack, you got this right here."

"Hey, like I know you can, Jackie. Like I know you can!"

On the fifth pitch of the at bat, Oklahoma's number five hitter connected with the ball and that all too familiar 'pop' came from her bat. She got the barrel, there was no doubt about that. I heard a scream come from the stands. My head jolted upward as my eyes followed the bright yellow softball through the dark night sky. Our right fielder, Jaz sprinted backwards to the edge of the grass and onto the warning track. It wasn't until her back was up against the wall that I saw her arm make a circular motion. "Mine!" she mouthed. The ball began to drop from the sky and eventually landed right into the webbing of Jaz's black glove. I will never forget the way Jaz and centerfielder, Jennifer Fenton celebrated that catch. Jaz outstretched both her arms above her head and had the biggest smile on her face. Jen's fist followed suit and jolted straight up into the air as she slowed her sprint, circled around, and high fived her fellow outfielder.

It was impossible to not lose yourself in a celebration during a game like this. As Jaz's arm flew into the air, I couldn't help but notice the faint glimmer of a red bandana laced in her glove's webbing. 'Our legacy is not done being written yet' I thought to myself. Onto the bottom of the fifth.

CHAPTER 14

"WHAT CAN I DO TO HELP MY TEAM TODAY?"

I can remember sitting in my senior individual meeting with the coaches in August of 2011. I still hadn't wrapped my mind around the fact that I was already a senior, where had these last few years gone? I looked down at the list of expectations the coaches handed to me. "Great expectations for CASSIE…" it read at the top. As always, the only number on the entire sheet was a target GPA for me to achieve. There was no pressure to achieve a certain batting average, number of homeruns, or slugging percentage. The only things written on each of our expectations were things the coaches truly felt I was in control of.

Number one on the sheet read, "Make your senior year about your teammates and it will be your best one yet!" This was the perfect expectation and it made so much sense to me as well as to the rest of my senior class. Each member of our senior class brought something to the table and we were able to compliment one another's weaknesses with our personal strengths. As individuals on the team, there always seemed to be something missing. We were not whole unless we were all operating on the same page as a unit. Had we not worked together, we would have been functioning at a level that was below our potential. However when together, with every leadership role we took on, we were able to accomplish something very special. We completed each other and we pushed each other to be at our best when we were surrounded by one another.

As a class we were entering our last year to play the sport we loved at the place we loved to play it. We were about to dive into a lot of 'lasts.' The last time running the conditioning test, last first practice, last fall ball season, etc. It is very easy to let this consume you as a senior. I've seen a lot of seniors beg and plead with their teammates to 'play for them' and 'give everything you have for us, your seniors, it's our last time!'

Starting the 2012 season, our class decided we didn't like the idea of that. We sat down as a group and tried to collectively come up with a way to avoid this mentality. Don't get me wrong, it is extremely flattering to have teammates push hard and say they are doing it for you. Or to hit a game winning hit and say it was for the seniors as they tried to extend their careers just one more game. Except, this wasn't just the senior's last year. This was Leslie Jury's first year, Jordan Patterson's second, and Kayla Braud's third. And the coaches sixteenth! This wasn't all about us as seniors; this was all about us as a team. When you sacrifice your body by diving for a ball in the gap, you don't sacrifice for any individual, you sacrifice for the *team*. The team is and always will be bigger than each of us alone. We played the game with enough emotion as it was, we didn't need the freshmen class getting over emotional thinking about trying to get a hit for the seniors while they were at the plate. That is not how we wanted it to happen. We wanted it all to be about us, and by 'us' I mean the team.

There was a mirror in our clubhouse prior to its renovation that had, "What can I do to help my team today?" written along the top. I loved that quote. I loved it even more that you saw it as you were looking at yourself in the mirror. If there was ever anything that wasn't going our way on the field, looking in that mirror and asking yourself what you could do to improve this team opposed to what everyone else could or should be doing, led to a very successful mentality.

We had a common theme on the team where we would compare our progress to the rowing of a boat. As individuals, there were going to be some days that our mental and physical fatigue was low and we felt fully capable of rowing the boat to help the team move forward. Other days, we may not have been able to row because of illness, injuries, or exhaustion. On those unfortunate days, our job was to take our oar out of the water and let our teammates carry us until we were able to row again. There was always something we could do to help the team improve. It was a constant challenge to not let the oar drag in the water which would make our teammates work extra hard in order to carry us along. We wanted to always be contributing, never resisting our collective progress.

For the 2012 season, the Alabama Softball senior class consisted of six members: Amanda Locke, Kendall Dawson, Jennifer Fenton, Jazlyn Lunceford, Olivia Gibson, and myself. As a class we wanted to embrace servant leadership. When I asked Olivia what her definition of a servant leader was she responded with, "A leader who sees empowering the team by placing the team's goals and other members first and themselves as a very distant second." We wanted to lead by serving our team. Urban Meyer, the championship head football coach for the Ohio State Buckeyes spoke in a press conference about the secret to any team he had been a part of that had found success. He said that it wasn't all about the workouts in the weight room or the number of plays they could run on offense and defense but instead it had everything to do with the internal leadership. Who on the team was going to hold their teammates accountable? Who was going to be passing along the ideals of the coaches to the rest of the team? It was those internal leaders who would be making the difference. I firmly believe if you have someone looking up to you then you are leader. That year, our team was filled with leaders. There were people who were younger than me that I looked up to in many ways. I also knew that I had people looking up to me as well. This was a responsibility, not a burden, and I felt every member of our team embraced their specific leadership role very well, especially our senior class.

Every year our coaches would ask us to come up with an intangible that we would bring to the table to make our team better. An intangible is defined as something that does not have a physical presence. Our coaches were not asking for how many homeruns we were going to hit or how many strikeouts the pitchers would have. They were asking for something that could not be measured or counted, something that you could contribute besides your stats. After everyone on the team had time to think about their intangible, we would state what we were going to bring to the table out loud in front of everyone. This allowed all members of the team to hear what your intangible was and put the responsibility on the team to hold each member accountable. After we shared, Whitney Larsen, our student assistant for the year, stood up at the front of the room and challenged us. She challenged us to not just bring these intangibles to the table for the first week or first month but for the entire season.

Amanda Locke's intangible for that year was to have the confidence of the best hitter in the country. This was not an easy task. Confidence was something that had to be worked at. There were many times that Amanda didn't necessarily *feel* like the most confident hitter in the country but she always *acted* like the best hitter in the country. This mentality ended up paying dividends at the end of the year. As mentioned earlier, Amanda went into a slump toward the beginning of playoffs. When she showed up at the WCWS she had not recorded a hit in the three weeks of post season so far. Still, she strutted to the box, tapped home plate with the end of her bat, brought her weapon into a loaded position on her right shoulder and stared down the opponent with an intensity and determination that screamed confidence. Without this, Amanda would have never been able to pull herself out of her slump. Amanda ended the World Series batting .333 with a homerun and five runs batted in. She was named to the WCWS All-Tournament team and was the source of three enormously clutch hits.

Kendall Dawson tasked herself with bringing a calming leadership presence while behind the plate. Catchers have the other eight positions on the field facing them during a game and Kendall took pride in being in this 'spotlight.' Throughout that entire season she played with the same intensity no matter the situation. There was never a moment bigger than her, Kendall's presence towered over any pressure packed situation. Jackie Traina pitched extremely well in 2012. Anyone who knows the sport of baseball or softball knows that behind every extraordinary pitcher there is an even better catcher.

Kendall was able to keep our pitcher calm even during the most adverse of situations. Kendall led us to a position to stay at an emotionally consistent level that became pertinent to our success when the stakes were highest.

'Having the determination to be the toughest out in the country' was what Jennifer Fenton declared her intangible to be. Jen ended up batting second in our lineup for the majority of the season. The responsibility of the number one batter is to get on base and set the tone for the entire game. This can be a high-pressure part of the lineup to bat in. What is even more arguably pressure filled is being the number two batter when the lead off did not get on. Jen handled this role like the true professional she was. No matter what Jen did in her previous ten at-bats, she never stopped making the opposing defense work hard. If the defense was playing tight for a bunt, she'd swing away. If they played middle distance for a slap, she'd bunt. And if they decided to play deep to defend her hitting then she'd have a number of ways to pick apart the defense and get on base. Not to mention, Jennifer Fenton broke the NCAA record with 74 consecutive stolen bases without being thrown out. All of her physical skills that made her an abnormal talent coupled with her determination to be a tough out led to an All-American season for her.

Jazlyn Lunceford committed to having a relentless fighter mentality. Anyone who has ever had the pleasure to watch Jaz compete on the field knows this was a perfect intangible for her. Jaz was the outfielder who would take off in a sprint at 100 mph and dive head first into a wall trying to go after a ball. She would never, ever give up on a play. Over and over again she would sacrifice her body in an attempt to make an out for her team. While at the plate, no ground ball would be an easy out for the defense. Once she hit the ball, she would tear out of the box with this ferocity that was impossible to replicate and with everything she had she would lunge her body through the bag, throwing her arms out to the side as to try and convince the umpire she was safe. Jaz never once left the field with a clean uniform. Sometimes even before the game started she would have already completed a head first dive into a muddy area of the outfield. It was her signature and what she was known for. 'Relentless fighter mentality' could have very well been her middle name.

Olivia Gibson was on a mission to bring pure joy to the team. She brought a genuine care and love for the game and her teammates that could not be denied. It was not fake, it was not a mask she could put on and take off, it was true and sincere. As the leader of the Wolfpack, she always did what was best for everyone else. Our team was able to feed off of her demeanor and even during times of struggle or adversity she was the source of reason. She had a way of sifting through the fog of anger in defeat and was able to find a positive for us all to latch onto to pull us through to the other side. She always seemed to know exactly what anyone needed in order to feel better. She was the foundation of comfort and peace and our constant reminder for how the game should be played.

My intangible for the 2012 season was to pour everything I had into my teammates. I wanted to pour my knowledge of the game into them and to never stop sharing different strategies for being successful on and off the field at Alabama. I felt I was fortunate enough to have had the opportunity to play with so many great teammates from the past years and I wanted to do nothing more than to pass on what I learned from them to my younger teammates. I wanted to share the same knowledge and passion that was given to me with every single one of them. I can remember being disappointed in the fall of 2011 that there were no potential first basemen on the team that were younger than me. I had wanted nothing more than to share everything I knew about the position I loved so much with someone else on the team. It was probably one of the happiest days of the season when Jadyn Spencer got sent from the outfield over to first base. I couldn't help but begin right away pouring everything I had into her.

That year, our senior class wanted to set up 'safety nets' for future teams in the program after we left. This meant sharing leadership roles. Something as simple as passing a task of talking in the huddle off to a junior or sophomore who would be expected to do so the following year would be beneficial for the entire team. We also made sure every person on the team understood what it meant to wear the script "A" on their chest, and what it truly meant to play softball at Alabama. This was the coolest thing to watch, I so enjoyed seeing every one in my class take on these various roles.

One concern I had coming into the 2012 season was that we had twenty girls on the team. This would be the largest team in Alabama Softball history. I was worried that a larger team could potentially lead to it being a bit more difficult to get all of us on the same page. However, number one on my list of expectations was the perfect tool that made getting everyone rowing in the same direction so easy.

As a senior class, we had been told since our freshman year that we 'got it' right away. But what did it mean to 'get it'? I think I can define it in two ways: 1. To genuinely care about the success of the team above your own. 2. Giving absolutely everything you have to give in order to help the team succeed. Three years earlier, when we were all freshman, wide-eyed and nervous about our next journey, we weren't thinking about trying to show everyone on the team that we had 'got it', we were simply just trying to find ways to help the team. That's why number one has 'genuine' written down. It is the foundation of 'getting it.' It's why you can't be taught to 'get it,' why 'getting it' can't be forced or coached. You either 'get it' or you don't.

Coach Aly spoke to us at a meeting one day. She took a stack of twenty papers and staggered them so that none of them were aligned with each other. She ripped all twenty pages in half as if it was nothing. She then staggered half the pages and aligned the other half. Still, every page tore right down the middle. Next she aligned fifteen of the pages and only left five staggered, although it was more difficult, the paper still ripped. Finally Aly aligned all twenty pages with one another and with all her might jolted the paper toward her with her right hand as she pushed the other side of the pages away from her with her left hand. She bent over and took the neatly aligned stack and pushed up against her waist using her leg as leverage to try and tear the pages. Her hands shook with furry as she gave the stack of pages everything she had to separate them. Still, the twenty aligned pages did not budge. She placed the pages down, looked at us all and said, "That is what it means to be on the same page. If all of you are on the same page, nothing will tear you a part and there will not be a team in the country that can beat you."

Back in the fall of 2008 when we were all freshman barely getting adjusted to the routine of being a student-athlete, we were all placed in a hitting group together. Coach Murphy was pitching batting practice to us while Aly was standing next to him behind the net. Murphy froze after Jennifer Fenton hit a line drive to the right center field gap. He turned his back to home plate, looked at Aly and said, "This class is going to win a National Championship their senior year." He then turned back around to face home plate and fired in another pitch to Jennifer Fenton. "Sounds good to me, Murph" Aly replied with a big smile on her face. She had never heard Murphy say anything like that about a player or a class.

I don't know how or why, but Murphy saw it in our class, something was special. I am still so thankful we ended up at Alabama at the right time. I can't even wrap my mind around how many things had to go right for us to all start our journeys together during that fall. We had to fall in love with the game at the right time, had to play on the right travel ball team, had to be in the right place at the right time to get recruited, and had to have that 'right' feeling to commit to Alabama. The list goes on and on, the stars truly aligned for us. I can't picture my life without any of my teammates, but especially my senior class. I would go through my four years at Alabama all over again just to walk hand in hand with them throughout our journey.

Our dream was to win it all, but in a sense we knew there would be a lot about that dream we could not control. Instead, we made a goal to not show our teammates how great we were but instead show them how great *they* were. We wanted to inspire them to be their best; to give full effort at all times, and to commit themselves to this team, the 2012 Alabama Crimson Tide softball team. If we did that, we knew the rest would take care of itself. We knew if we did that, we would never struggle to sleep at night. We could lay our heads on our pillow knowing we gave all of ourselves to them. And if the end result worked out the way we had hoped, we would no longer have to dream at night to feel what the celebration might be like, we'd know.

"20 on 1, 20 on 1."

We chanted this over and over as our batter, Jennifer Fenton stood in the box. We wanted to remind her that she was never alone. Jen reached first safely on a bunt base hit to lead things off for us.

We made a commitment earlier in the year that we would never practice or play just to beat the other team. We were constantly trying to match our team's best performance. We still believed that we had not played our best game yet and were trying to do so in that championship game.

Jen advanced to second base on a wild pitch to Kaila Hunt. Kaila then did one of the most selfless things you will ever see happen on a baseball or softball field. It will never end up in the paper or on the scoreboard. She hit a ground ball to the second baseman to advance Jen to third base. I know it doesn't seem like much but it is an extremely important detail to the game. With a runner on second base and no outs, your job as a hitter is to get the runner to third. By hitting a ground ball to the right side, you are doing your job but you are getting zero credit for it. It doesn't count as a sacrifice or a hit, it counts as an out. You did your job perfectly but will never get acknowledgment in the stats book for it. However, our teammates knew where credit was due. Our team met Kaila outside the dugout with high fives and pats on the helmet. She was the first person to lead us all back into the dugout after the entire team had congratulated her. The details mattered big time.

A hard hit ball to right field by Jackie Traina scored Jen and our lead grew by two runs. This was such an important run. Anyone who has ever played knows the difference between a one run lead and the cushion of a two run lead.

In the top of the sixth inning Jackie made quick work of the Oklahoma hitters. She looked as if she was getting stronger as the game *went on. Her accuracy at this point in the game was astonishing as she was closing in on her 800th pitch of the World Series.*

In the bottom of the sixth inning we weren't able to get anything going. I paced up and down the dugout telling everyone to stay in the present. If we wanted to finish this thing, we would have to do so one pitch at a time. No matter the situation, the game would always be the same. It is always softball. The only thing that changes the game is the way we react to the added pressures. If someone were to lay a plank of wood on the ground in front of you and tell you to walk across it, you would do so without hesitation, without any doubt that you could make it across. Now, if that person then elevated that plank ten feet into the air and then told you to walk across it, you might not be so confident that you could make it all the way across. The plank is the exact same distance and the exact same width as the one you strolled across so nonchalantly on the ground. The task itself hasn't become any more difficult, but the stakes have gotten higher. This is how it feels to play in the World Series. It's the same exact game you've always played, with the same exact rules, but this time, if you lose your balance the fall is that much further. By keeping focused and locked in on one pitch at a time, we were able to wash those pressures away. We were going to play Alabama Softball no matter the situation. One step at a time, slowly and confidently across the plank we knew so well.

On to the top of the seventh inning. As I ran back onto the field, there were no more thoughts that flashed through my mind. No thoughts of this being the last time I'd run to my position or the last time to take the field as a member of the Tide. No thoughts of celebrating or blowing the lead. My only thoughts were in the here and now. I looked over at Jack as she finished her warm-up pitches.

"You know we're in that circle with you on every pitch."

She smirked and said, "Oh, I know."

"You feel it Jack?" I asked.

Another smile. She looked calm. "Yeah, I can feel it."

Doubt had no room. Fear was not welcomed. The top of the order would be coming to the plate for Oklahoma. The first batter of the inning hit a sharp ground ball that was fielded by third baseman, Courtney Conley and thrown to first for the initial out of the inning.

"Hey one down, one down, way to work, Jack. Way to work."

The next batter came to the plate. She too was a lefty slap hitter. She slapped a pitch from Jackie that bounced along the first base line. As I went to field the ground ball I realized the runner's approach to first base and my approach to the ball would have to intersect.

Rewind to my freshman year. We played Mississippi State in the first SEC match up of the year. A similar ball was hit by a slapper down the first base line and instead of fielding the ball, I adjusted my path in order to get out of the way of the runner. The runner ended up being safe at first. The coaching staff after the game made sure I knew the rule. They made sure I knew that I, as the fielder, had a right to the ball and that if the runner was in fair territory, any contact made with her would result in interference on the runner and an automatic out. I nodded wide-eyed as a freshman thinking I fully understood the rule. This is what makes Alabama the great program it is with consistent success. The coaching staff made sure I <u>really</u> understood the rule. The very next practice we had, I ran that play over and over again. This is such a tiny detail of the game yet the coaches saw it as vitally important. That play did not happen once again in my entire career at Alabama. Not until this batter. Not until the final inning of my final game in my career. Chopped hard by the slapper, the ball ricocheted off the packed infield dirt along the first base line. As I ran to field the ball, I quickly realized the runner was directly in my path. Contact was inevitable. As her cleats landed in fair territory, I knew what I had to do, I had learned the rule. I braced my body for the impact. After the play was over, a brief meeting amongst the umpires declared the runner was out. Bottom of the seventh, two outs.

"Keep working, Jack! Let's finish this thing!"

The third batter of the inning stepped up to the plate. She had already hit a homerun earlier in the game. On Jackie's 788th pitch of the World Series, the Oklahoma batter hit another one. It was a no doubter over the centerfield fence. Oklahoma had pulled within one run. There was something different about this homerun though. My left eardrum didn't explode this time. Oklahoma's celebration at home plate didn't appear the same. Before they celebrated and cheered as if they were sure they were going to win. Now, it seemed like they were wavering, doubt had crept in.

After the homerun our infield huddled up around Jackie.

"Hey, clean slate right here."

"Yeah, one pitch at time, Jack."

"No worries, let's finish it strong."

"Hey let's get one, on three, 1,2,3"

The small huddle of infielders replied with, "Get one."

'Get one.' As if this 'one' was just another batter in the season. As if this 'one' didn't stand as the potential final out of the game, final out of the season, final out standing between us and the one thing we wanted most, a National Championship. The next batter coming to the plate for Oklahoma was the national player of the year. She too had hit a homerun earlier in the game. The first pitch from Jackie was a strike on the outside corner. The second pitch was an off speed pitch that was swatted at by the hitter's bat. The ball came off the bat down the right field line and into foul territory. I fielded the foul ball and rubbed the bright yellow softball with my left hand to see if it was dry. The noise of the excitement in the stands faintly echoed in my ear. I looked up at Jackie and said calmly, "Nice job, Jack, let's get this <u>one</u> right here."

On the third pitch of the at-bat, Jackie hurled the ball toward home plate. Kendall caught the 70mph outside drop ball and framed it perfectly. Her glove barely moved.

'That looked like a strike.' I thought to myself. Then I saw the hand. The umpire's right hand, it went straight up into the air as she uncurled from her crouched stance.

That means strike three.

That means out number three.

That means we won.

I leapt off my tightrope. I threw my hands in the air. I yelled as loudly as I could and I ran. I ran for my team. I could no longer control my thoughts or actions. I just wanted to get to my teammates so badly. I wanted to experience this celebration, this moment. I wanted to hold onto it and never let it go. I was no longer balanced on my tightrope. I lost control of everything and fell and landed in the best dog pile imaginable. I landed among my teammates, my best friends, my family. I held onto them like I was never going to let go. We did it. There was nothing else to accomplish, nothing left to win. We won it all, we won it all, we won it all.

CHAPTER 15

"FINISH IT."

Every year we had a theme. It was always something that directly applied to the personality, character, and goals of the team that year. For the 2012 season, our theme was to 'finish it.' In the fifteen year history of the Alabama Softball program, the team had reached the Women's College World Series seven times. Of the previous four years leading up to the 2012 season, Alabama had made the semi-final round three times. Still, there were no appearances in the championship series for the Tide and no national championships to show. Although making it to the WCWS and coming in third are all stats to be extremely proud of, the coaching staff and players were not satisfied. Coach Murphy and the team had knocked on the door time and time again but the final victory had always eluded the Tide...Until now.

In our first meeting of the 2012 season, our new pitching coach, Stephanie VanBrakle was introduced to us. We were all very familiar with Steph. She was a former All-American star-pitcher in her playing days at Alabama. The very first thing she said in the meeting was that she was ready to win this whole thing. She had tried four times as a player and was so thankful to be able to come back and have an opportunity to finish it one more time. Until now, Steph had believed that her chance at a national title was nothing more than a dream of the past. After her senior year, the flame of hope to win the WCWS had been extinguished. As she spoke to us that day, chills draped across my entire body. I could see that that flame had never really gone out for her. The embers had still been there all along. Burning hot and red and after all this time, they were ready to be ignited once again. There was something about her demeanor, tone, and facial expressions. We all knew she meant business. Steph was a competitor to her core and we were all elated to have someone like her as one of our leaders.

Strength and conditioning coach Michelle Diltz came to the front of the clubhouse to speak in that meeting as well. "We have knocked on the door time and time again. I am sick of knocking on the door. I hope y'all are ready because I am ready to bust through." Our team was engrossed with every word she said. If Michelle was not defeated by near misses of the previous years, neither would we. The tone for our season would be set in the weight room and she was ready to help us make it happen. On paper, her job made her the one responsible for making sure we were in peak physical shape to perform at our best when we were on the field. What may not have been in her official job description is what she was able to get us to accomplish during those strength and conditioning sessions. She was the one who was able to get us to push past what we all thought was our 'limit.' I can remember many times feeling sweat pour down my face as if a bucket of water had just been dumped over my head. My legs screamed with fatigue and my breathing strained, praying for a break. "Come on, ladies!"

That was all it took. Michelle's voice. It was enough to make the ache and the strain go away. She was able to get us to do something we otherwise did not think was possible. She gave us a workout and she never showed an ounce of doubt that we wouldn't be able to complete it. Michelle provided an environment designed to bind us closer together in an attempt to accomplish our end of year goal.

Any team that has won National Championships, World Series, Super Bowls, and Stanley Cups did not just win these championships on the last day of the season. They won these trophies in the days, weeks, and months leading up to that final game. Our 'end' was to win it all, to finally finish it. We made a commitment to train every day with the 'end' in mind. Each day we trained and practiced to win a national championship, not just to get 'through' the work out.

To 'Finish it' is a process. It is a certain mentality that encompasses every aspect of the season. If we expected to finish the season strong and be at our best when it mattered the most in the final game of the year, we were going to have to practice it. To us, finishing it meant making sure every time we warmed up, we finished through the line and not a single step before. It meant making sure our last rep of a set was our most explosive and powerful rep of the day. That our last set was also our best set. We were always trying to find a way to match our best and then surpass it. Finishing it meant that even when we were exhausted during the last five minutes of a lift, a conditioning session, or a practice, we were going to discipline ourselves to make those last five minutes as close to flawless as humanly possible. When it came time for the end of the season we wanted to be pressing the gas pedal trying to accelerate at top speed through the finish line, not crawling exhausted and out of breath.

The end of the game is when you are the most exhausted. The end of the season is when you fight the roughest fatigue. The seventh inning is when the pitcher's legs start getting tired. Come playoffs is when our bodies ache more and more each time we wake up in the morning. It's when we are at our weakest that we must find a way to play and perform at our best. In order to practice this, it takes an abnormal level of focus. It requires demanding a higher level of excellence out of yourself and your team, not just at the end of the season, but during every day leading up to the end. It's all about finding a way to finish a play, finish a practice, and finish a season strong.

In the fall of 2011 we all made a commitment to focusing on one thing to get better at each week. We knew what our 'outcome goals' were. They were listed on the top of a piece of paper; we wanted to win the SEC tournament, the SEC regular season, and lastly the National Championship. However, wanting to accomplish all of these things was not enough, we needed a road map to get there, a way to stay focused on what it was going to take to achieve the goals we had set for ourselves. Written below our goals on that sheet of paper was the question, "How are we going to get there?" There were four weeks of practice that fall; each week represented an opportunity to improve on one aspect of our game. We picked out four specific goals to focus on. Four factors of our game that we could control that would help us fulfill our ultimate goal, to finally 'finish it.'

For week one we met as a team on our own ten minutes before the start of our Tuesday practice. That first week we committed to getting better at communicating on the field. We picked out four to five people on our team to lead us that week at getting better at communication. As a team we agreed two of those players were very strong at communicating and set a great example for our team to follow. The other two to three members of that group were players who needed to get better at communicating in order for us to be successful that year. This is not an easy conversation to have. A team must be very honest with one another and feel very safe in that environment in order to say, "I think you need to get better at this in order for us to win a national championship." Those core group of four to five people were responsible for getting our entire team better at communicating that first week of fall ball. Whether we improved or didn't improve that week was on them. Each week that we felt like we improved, we were able to give those core group of people the credit for leading us one step closer to our goals. We were putting people in a position to lead, a position to learn, and a position to feel responsible for our success as a team.

The second week we made a point to focus on all-out effort. We strove to compete with a reckless abandon. A type of effort that made the jaws of people in the stands watching us for the first time drop to the ground. The third week was all about paying attention to the details. It called for focusing on the tiny aspects of the game and making sure we were not leaving any rock unturned. Finally, the forth week encompassed everything it meant to truly finish it. For that final week of practice we focused on achieving a higher level of greatness. Whenever we dove for a ball, it wasn't good enough to let it hit our glove and pop out. We were going to find a way to finish the play. It was no longer good enough to just give max effort on the play. We were demanding something more. We were demanding to finish with quality and excellence. 'Good enough' was no longer good enough. Only a genuine excellence was going to cut it. It was no longer enough to just make it to the World Series. It was no longer satisfactory to come in third place. We were ready to finish with conviction and greatness. We were ready to become the first team from the University of Alabama to win the Women's College World Series. We were ready to be the first team from the Southeastern Conference to win it all. We were ready to finish it.

With this mentality I began to recognize a change in the way we spoke to one another at practices and during games. When someone didn't get the bunt down, no one said, 'It's okay,' instead, 'Make it happen,' 'Find a way,' and 'Finish the play' were commonly heard on the diamond. We expected more out of ourselves and from each other, and that carried over to the off-field mentality as well. Our team that year made the best decisions off the field out of any team I had ever been a part of. I don't believe there is a coincidence between these decisions and our end of season success.

As a team we wanted a constant reminder of what we were trying to do every practice and every game. With big help from our media department at Alabama we were able to come up with a sign. It was a square, one foot by one foot poster that had a dark crimson background. Across the middle of the poster were the words, "FINISH IT." My favorite part of the sign was the dirt stained handprint smeared across the bottom. It was located right next to the door in our hitting facility. Every single day when we would walk out onto the field for a practice or a game, we would have that as our daily reminder. It was something we could touch right before we left for battle. It stood for something that would hold us accountable to obtain our goal. Our media department was even nice enough to make us a portable travel sign that we could have on the road with us. By the time that poster got to Oklahoma City it had been sat on, stepped on, splattered with mud, rain, and faded from sunshine. It was worn but at the same time, so was our team. That is exactly why we made 'finish it' our theme in the first place. We knew this was how we were going to be at the end of the season, and we worked tirelessly and endlessly to find a way to play at our best when we did not necessarily feel at the height of our game.

Toward the end of the season, teammate Jordan Patterson left all of us a present on our stools in the locker room before we played the Florida Gators in a decisive SEC championship game. Laying on our stool were thick black wristbands that had the words, "FINISH IT" in white block lettering. They were the perfect symbol and reminder for us to wear for the rest of our journey. It served as our constant reminder of the task at hand.

Our coaches would always remind us that our season was a marathon and not a sprint. It is a long grueling season that can take a lot out of you. A sprinter's race is short, an all out burst of intensity. Although this exertion may leave them winded, they are quick to recover. Their race did not drain the tank dry. However, when a marathon runner crosses the finish line, they have kept pace for 26.2 miles, every step of the way disciplining themselves to maintain stamina, speed, and determination. They push through steady and consistent. Without the finish line in sight, their focus is on each individual step, each one bringing them closer and closer to their goal. We had to look at our season from the same perspective. There were many steps to take before that finish line was in sight. One at a time, we tackled each mile of our own marathon, game-by-game, inning-by-inning, pitch-by-pitch. When we reached our finish line, we would cross it tank depleted, every single reserve run dry.

What does it truly mean to finish it? It means having been battle tested and accustomed to finding a way to play at your best when you are at your worst and the fuel gauge is at its lowest. It allows you to be at your strongest come playoffs when it is natural and 'logical' to be at your weakest. It means knowing how to take a look inside yourself and ask, "What more can I give today to help my team?" It requires you to dig deeper so that when you make it to Oklahoma City for the WCWS, you are confident because of your persistent preparation. It means having a heightened sense of what it takes to be extraordinary and what it requires to be excellent in the face of adversity. Practicing what it takes to finish it means when it comes time for the final pitch of the national championship game, you're more than ready. It means having visualized yourself finding success over and over again that when the opportunity presents itself to be legendary, you'll be ready and as a result, you'll finally be able to finish it.

CHAPTER 16

"KEEP YOUR FORKS!"

In the fall of my freshman year, the theme for the 2008-2009 Alabama softball team was already decided. "Keep Your Forks" was imprinted on the shirts handed to all five seniors that year. Coach Murphy told a story from his childhood about eating dinner at his grandmother's home. At the very end of dinner, young Coach Murphy would sit and wait with anticipation, watching his grandmother's every move. He was hoping to hear his favorite phrase come out of her mouth as she cleared the plates off of the dinner table. Once he heard, "Keep your forks!" he knew something bigger and better was coming his way; dessert. Our coaches told our senior class that year that no matter how things have gone in the past, no matter the letdowns and failures, they needed to keep their forks for this year, because something better was coming their way.

When Jackie Traina came on her unofficial recruiting visit in the fall of 2008, she learned of the teams theme for that year. When she decided to verbally commit to Alabama, Jackie sent a small box to Coach Murphy. When Murphy opened the box there was a list of all of Jackie's favorite desserts that included key-lime pie and banana pudding. Underneath the list of desserts, tucked away at the bottom of a box was a fork. A fork for Murphy to keep in anticipation of Jackie arriving at Alabama.

The phrase, "Keep your forks" has lots of parallels to life. It's about always looking forward to something even better about to come. During that 2012 season, we often said, "Today will either be better or worse than yesterday, but it will never be the same." Still to this day, that quote constantly challenges us to find a way to make the day we were presented with better than the day before. Finding a way to make the week, month, year, or circumstance we find ourselves in better than what ever has already occurred in the past. This is a decision we must make every day regardless if we are a student, athlete, coach, friend, daughter, mother, etc. Outside circumstances, such as other people, the weather, or things that are out of our control should never dictate our day. Our response to everything we cannot control lies in our ability to make all of our todays better than our yesterdays.

Winning the national championship was one of the most amazing experiences of my life. However, I know that it won't be the best of life because I know the best is always yet to come. No matter where you are in your sport know that something bigger and better is in store for you. Even if you are injured, understand that the best days are ahead for you once you are finally healthy. If you have just lost the last game of the season, know that only by experiencing the low from a loss will you truly be able to appreciate the high from a win. Even now that I am done playing, no matter how much I miss competing, how much I miss being a part of a team, I know that my best experiences in life are ahead of me. Wake up excited for the 'dessert' that may come your way on any given day. I try and challenge myself daily to keep my fork because I know that the actual dessert isn't always the best part of life. Instead, the anticipation and excitement for what might come next is truly what is worth looking forward to.

I know that playing this game can sometimes be difficult. Especially as a student athlete, a lot is placed on your plate. It can sometimes challenge our love for the game. It can make us wonder why we signed up for this in the first place and why we continue to push ourselves to do this. Why we committed to the long hours of practice, the early morning workouts, the spring breaks and summer vacations filled not with pools and trips to the beach but instead dedicated to playing in tournaments and games. Being dedicated and committed requires you to forfeit being a 'normal' teenager or a 'normal' college student. I know it can all add up and it can be tough. However, this can all be overcome by staying focused on keeping your forks day in and day out.

AFTERWARD

I have a challenge for anyone who plays this game and every athlete who decides to make a commitment to it. I challenge you to become the best you can possibly be. To put forth your best effort you can put forth. To sign away every fiber of your being to the game you fell in love with. I challenge you to never stop finding new ways to fall in love with this sport and to constantly remind yourself why this is all more than worth it.

I challenge you to look at this game in its purest form. Take away the coach that insults you and embarrasses you, the parent that obsesses over every move, and the teammate that sucks the positive energy from you. Wash it all away. Try to take away the injuries, the sore and aching body and scrapes and bruises. Playing this game can be a thankless job. The game can beat you down time and time again with its never-ending adversities and challenges. However, it is your love for this game that will hold fast. I promise you our game knows. Our game knows when it is loved, it knows when it is studied, and it knows when someone is working tirelessly at it. This game will reward you. Understand that the 'reward' is not necessarily hoisting a trophy at the end of the season. Realize that the true prize lies in experiencing some of the most fulfilling moments of your life. And that by meeting coaches and teammates that will make you a better person in life is one of the greatest gifts this game can reward you with.

Approach a field and look at this game from a child's eyes. Go look at an empty field while it is lit up at night. A field with the green grass cut, the infield raked over, the foul lines freshly chalked, and the white bases cleanly spray-painted. Cover your face with your glove and take a deep breath in, smell the leather and the dirt and appreciate how many fields that glove has been imprinted by. Pick up a bat with your bare hands and feel it's grip, how the handle nestles perfectly against your callused hands. Listen closely to what your cleats sound like as you walk onto the infield.

Take a look at the way a base runner sprints as they try and score from first to home on a ball hit in the gap. Admire the look in their eyes as they glance at their third base coach waving them home, how their eyes light up with determination and grit. Or the way an outfielder tears after a ball that no one thinks they have any chance of getting. The hustle that goes into their sprint, the athleticism and effort that goes into their dive, and finally, admire their pride when they raise their glove triumphantly with the ball securely lodged in it's webbing.

Take a look into a pitcher's eyes, in the bottom of the seventh with two outs, the bases loaded and her team up by one run. You'll see a look that says, "There is no way this hitter will be successful." Then take a glance at the hitter as she digs in with her cleats in the batter's box determined to prove that pitcher wrong.

After we won our last game, it didn't make not having softball a part of our every day life easy. Maybe it was easier because we ended our careers with a 'W,' but it was by no means a walk in the park. Every one of us missed something about the game. It was still very obvious to me when I woke up in the morning that I was no longer a member of the Crimson Tide Softball team. Until this day, I still haven't had the heart to wipe away, "What can I do to help my team today?" from the top of my mirror. I was no longer giving everything I had for the team. That weight of responsibility that says you are a part of something so much bigger than yourself was no longer with my every move throughout the day. That was a difficult adjustment to make.

The other seniors and I would joke that if we could go back for just one day to relive it all again how great it would be. To relive a day out of our freshman year when we were all first getting to know each other or the celebration after a walk off homerun. Just to experience one more time the chills we got when the Oklahoma City announcer boomed at Hall of Fame Stadium, "Your 2012 NCAA Division I National Champions, the Alabama Crimson Tide!" Amanda Locke would often call or text me, jokingly request that I start mastering time travel. Every now and then I'll still get a text, "How's that time machine coming, Cass?" Well guess what, Locke? Here is the time machine, it is finally complete. This book is for us. It is for our team that will forever walk together, hand in hand as the 2012 National Champions. No matter what records may be broken, we will always have our spot cemented in history. Perhaps this book can be our way of going back and reliving some of the great memories we were all able to make together. It can remind us all of the hard work and determination it took for us to accomplish such a feat. It can serve to reinforce the idea that we are capable of anything we want in our lives, if there is something we set out to do, we will be successful. Just because our time as a member of the Crimson Tide has passed, it doesn't change our mindset of constantly pursuing greatness in everything we do.

Thank you all for a season that changed my life. This book is for each and every one of you.

-Cassie Reilly-Boccia #18
Alabama Softball 2009-2012

ACKNOWLEDGEMENTS

During my sophomore year in college I was asked to write a one-page paper about something I believed in. The instructions were open ended and I sat and thought about this particular assignment for a while. I finally came up with one word that I felt encompassed who I was: appreciation. I firmly believe that my ability to appreciate the life I have is the key to a happy and successful time spent on Earth. I wish I had the space to list everyone who has influenced me in writing this book. Every person who has crossed paths with me in my lifetime has helped mold me into a better version of myself. My grandmother once told me that ones blessings are the true measure of a person's wealth, not their car, house, or job. If that is the case, then I consider myself wealthy beyond belief.

There are a few people in particular that I would like to give a special thanks to. Thank you to my parents for without hesitation jumping on board with me for every dream I have ever had. To all of my aunts, uncles, and awesome cousins for your never-ending support. The excitement you shared with me during this process has made it all the more special. Thank you to Grandpa for introducing me to this amazing game and teaching me how special it was. Thank you to Bridgette Quimpo for convincing me to write this book and constantly reassuring me that I could do this. To Rob Crews for the extreme wisdom and unique insight you share with me about this game. Special thanks to Alyson Habetz for filling me with endless hope and continuing to inspire me on a daily basis. Thank you to Coach Murphy for all of your teachings. You took pride in making us better people before athletes and I can never thank you enough for that. To Emily Pitek Clifford for being my set of 'fresh eyes' and filling me with hope and excitement about the future of these stories. Thank you to the entire staff that worked the grounds and stadium at the Rhoads house. There is a reason why people say that stadium is the best place to play in college softball and it starts with all of you. Thank you to the Alabama faithful for all of the encouragement and motivation throughout rain or shine. Thank you to the girls I have the privilege to coach in Alabama, Iowa, and New York. Each and every one of you has played a role in providing inspiration and guidance for this book. Thank you to Cup of Joe coffee house in Cedar Falls, Iowa for the perfect environment to write a book and the best pumpkin mocha latte I've ever had. Thank you to my mentors that I look up to on a daily basis: Dr. Robin Lund, Dr. Travis Ficklin, Nicholas Serio, Adam Arbour, Steph VanBrakle, Kate Harris, Kristin and Mr. Meister, Nick Seiler, Michelle Diltz, and Dr. Jeff Laubenthal. Thank you to Brittany Mayweather for being an amazing light in my life, asking me to be a god-mother, and cheering me on every step of the way throughout this entire process. Thank you to Jones for your excited encouragement throughout all of this. Thank you to Tom Dumser for all of your help during this (what seemed to be never-ending) process, you have one of the purest hearts that is constantly pursuing ways to help others. Thank you to my grandma…for just being you, may you rest peacefully and continue to shine your light down from Heaven. Huge thanks goes to Katie Bress for being by my side through it all and painstakingly going through every single word of this book with me. Not everyone is so lucky as to have someone in their life that knows their thoughts better than they do. And thank you to my mom for doing the same and going through this book several times, reading each word over and over with me. Thank you to Chris for being my mom and mines voice of reason. Finally, thank you to the team, coaches, and support staff for everything, this book does not exist without you: Patrick Murphy, Alyson Habetz, Stephanie VanBrakle, Adam Arbour, Whitney Larsen, Kate Harris, Michelle Diltz, Nick Seiler, Ashley Legget, Tim Osterhoudt, Addy Hamilton, Jordan Burson, Russel Larsen, Miles Snider, Chandler Whidden, Kendall Dawson, Jennifer Fenton, Olivia Gibson, Amanda Locke, Jazlyn Lunceford, Jackey Branham, Kayla Braud, Courtney Conley, Keima Davis, Lauren Sewell, Kaila Hunt, Ryan Iamurri, Jordan Patterson, Jaclyn Traina, Chaunsey Bell, Danae Hays, Lelsie Jury, Danielle Richard, Jadyn Spencer, Chris England, Chad Haynie, Nathan Kogut, Dr. Jeff Laubenthal, Scott Moyer, Jason Nance, Skip Powers, Marie Robbins, and Ashley Waters.

And as always, Roll Tide.